FINTECH

Financial Services

Dr. Madhuri Ashok Kadam
Assistant Professor
Bharati Vidyapeeth (Deemed to be) University,
Department of Management Studies (Off campus),
Kharghar, Navi Mumbai.
Contact No. 9833406813
Email Id: Madhuri.kadam@bharatividyapeeth.edu

Made with ❤ on the Notion Press Platform
www.notionpress.com

CONTENTS

CHAPTER 1

UNDERSTANDING FINTECH

1.1 DEFINITION

Fintech is the creative use of technology in financial design and delivery. It is based on key technologies: mobile applications, blockchain, AI, and big data analytics-finally offering an efficient, user-friendly, and safe financial solution to handle their financial transactions. Fintech means dealing with customers and companies without the great need for huge banking infrastructures in managing financial transactions.

Financial technology encompasses a wide range of services, from online banking and mobile payments to digital lending, robot-advisory services, and even insurance tech. By automating several processes, fintech enhances not only operational efficiency but also customer experience by making financial services accessible 24/7 through digital platforms.

The most important field in which it has left a mark is that of digital payment. Payment service providers like PayPal, Google Pay, and Apple Pay have completely revolutionized the mode of payment of people for goods and services. It has facilitated instant money transfer across different parts of the world. In addition to that, the fintech-powered wallet has provided an opportunity for the unbanked populations of different developing countries to take part in the formal economy and hence drove financial inclusion at a global level.

With innovative influence diffusing into practically all directions, blockchain represents one of the most revolutionary fintech innovations thoughts at the heart of Bitcoin and Ethereum cryptocurrencies. Those function based on the very promise of highly transparent and secure modes of dealing, verifying, and bookkeeping of transactions in a completely decentralized manner. This very technology is applied to manifold fields other than virtual cryptocurrency: supply chain management, healthcare record management, and even the implementation of smart contracts.

Fintech has innovatively changed the investment and wealth management segment by integrating financial services. AI-powered robot-advisors like Betterment and Wealth front provide algorithm-driven personalized financial advice to bring more accessibility for management of investments. Insights driven by data from Fintech applications help the businesses in decision-making, optimization of portfolios, and risk management effectively, thus letting Fintech set a place considered for changing modern finance.

Accessibility has increased, and this has been one of the major reshaping factors in the financial services landscape. Traditional banking was confined to coming to the branch, filling out much paperwork, and then waiting in line to be served. Fintech comes in by turning all these activities on their head through online banking, mobile payment systems, and instant loan approvals. For instance, platforms like Paytm and Venmo have innovatively made it possible to transfer cash in real time without needing cash or checks. This makes financial services even accessible in the most remote and undeserved areas, hence fostering financial inclusion around the globe.

The other major advantage of FinTech is affordability. Automating all the key processes, such as underwriting loans, processing payments, and performing compliance checks, financial technology cuts costs not only for those offering financial services but also the consumers. Through digital platforms like Stripe and Square, cost-effective solutions are offered to businesses. Usually, most of the savings accrue to the consumers who can get financial services at a cheap rate.

Fintech has revolutionized the industry with an enhanced customer experience. Given the great expectations of modern consumers, high-level personalization related to services will mean efficiency. Certain robo-advisors, such as Betterment and Wealthfront, provide their customers with customized investment portfolios that align with an investor's financial goals through their algorithms. Budgeting apps like Mint and YNAB track a user's personal spending, set up savings goals, and remind them for streamlined financial management.

Key areas of support for the growth of fintech include an increase in security. Advanced encryption protocols, biometric authentication, and real-time fraud detection systems make these transactions way more secure. Blockchain provides a decentralized, immutable ledger system that enables close-to-tamper-proof transactions, thus allowing safe and transparent transactions in a decentralized manner. For example, Zelle is one of the digital payment services that deploy bank level security protocols to ensure safe transfer of funds from one account to another within minutes.

For instance, fintech brought disruptive change to the online payment fraternity through its seamless, safe and globally accepted transaction platform. Initial PayPal, that kicked off as an online auction payment service has grown to be one of the global fintech firms. It might be because it has a very friendly user interface, and above all, fraud protection systems integrated in many ways to make sure online shopping is convenient but secure for millions of users.

1.2 DEVELOPMENT OF FINANCIAL SERVICES

The journey of fintech describes the infusion of technology into the financial service industry. There are some monumental events that have transformed how offering services actually takes place in this space.

1.2.1 The Pre-Internet Era

Spanning the 1960s to 1990s, laid the foundational elements of modern Fintech through developments such as ATMs, credit cards, and EFTs. ATMs. have been very instrumental in changing the way banking is conducted by enabling customers to have access to cash and account balances at any given time, reducing dependence on physical bank branches. On the other hand, credit cards including Visa and MasterCard facilitated non-cash transactions and boosted international trade. Mainframe computers also made banking operations faster because they automated back-office jobs of transaction processing and bookkeeping.

1.2.2 Internet Boom (1990s-2000s)

In the age of the Internet Boom the internet permeated financial services. First, there appeared online banking when all transactions, bill payments and money transfers became possible to conduct without leaving a bank. In came PayPal in 1998 to pioneer digital payments through online money transfers-one of the very first success stories of FinTech. E*TRADE also innovated stock trading to the level where persons were able to trade in stocks while enjoying the comfort of their homes, hence affording access to more and more people the opportunity for the stock market. During the Mobile and Digital Transformation, mobile devices and internet connectivity drove the rapid growth of fintech services in the 2000s-2010s. Mobile payment solutions such as Apple Pay, Google Pay, and Samsung Pay allowed users to make contactless payments through their smartphones, changing the way people shopped daily. Peer-to-peer lending platforms, such as Lending Club, allowed individuals to borrow and lend money directly to each other, bypassing banks. This was also the time when digital banking began to crop up, with a number of fintech startups offering purely online banking to tech-savvy clients.

1.2.3 The Current Era

The 2010s to the Present Day Moved on a Path of Innovation-Blockchain, Cryptocurrencies, and DeFi. Blockchain technology offers security, transparency, and tamper-proof transactions, alongside the development of cryptocurrencies like Bitcoin and Ethereum. Moreover, decentralized finance platforms enable lending, borrowing, and trading in the absence of intermediaries. Artificially intelligent-powered tools also changed the way investment management was done until now. Robo-advisors can now provide personalized financial counsel based on complex algorithms with big data analytics.

Example: The mobile wallet and digital banks have changed the way that the world perceives banks. It allows one individual to pay another in an easy way, and transactions are as easy as a text message. It provides borderless banking: multi-currency accounts, low-cost foreign exchange rates, and trading in cryptocurrency-redefining global banking services.

1.3 KEY DRIVERS OF FINTECH GROWTH

This phenomenal growth of FinTech has been made possible by a set of key drivers that have completely reshaped the financial landscape. They fuel innovation, enhance accessibility, and respond to changing needs from both sides: the consumers and businesses.

1.3.1 Technological Advancements

Fintech core incorporates several new technologies, including Artificial Intelligence, Blockchain, Big Data, and Mobile technologies, which enhance financial services to a completely different level: making financial systems way quicker, more secure, but all the same, very much accessible.

Artificial Intelligence and Machine Learning: Powering Personalization and Transforming Security

AI and ML have emerged to be very important tools in reshaping the operations of financial institutions; they scan gigantic datasets in real time, identify patterns, and make predictions, thus improving decision-making and service delivery.

- **Fraud Detection:** AI-powered systems monitor transactions at all times to detect anomalies. Such suspicious activities will show unusual spending habits, including location-based discrepancies. In that case, it flags threats even before they spiral beyond one's control and keeps the loss of money contained.
- **Risk Assessment:** The algorithms of Machine Learning review all non-traditional credit points like utility payments, social media, and transaction history to provide a better estimate of the probability of repayment by borrowers with no traditional credit history.
- **Personalized Financial Services:** AI-powered robo-advisors can make customized investment recommendations based on financial objectives, risk tolerance, and consumption patterns. For instance, a beginner investor may be advised about low-risk mutual funds, while for an advanced investor, advice might be given concerning stocks or cryptocurrencies.

Example: AI-driven chatbots can support customers 24/7, respond to queries, process loan applications, and even disputes on their own without human interference, ensuring a seamless user experience.

Blockchain Technology: Enhancement in Transparency and Security

Blockchain technology is the redefinition of trust for financial transactions. In other words, it is an immutable and decentralized ledger system whereby every transaction is recorded as a block, then encrypted and added to a chain, thus making it tamper-proof and very secure.

- **Transparency:** Whatever transactions are in process within a blockchain network, both parties will have the same set of transactions; hence, error variance is eradicated and tracking is possible.

- **Fraud Reduction:** Since blockchain is decentralized, no one controls the data, and there will hardly be fraud.
- **Simplification of Processes:** This has allowed streamlining of processes, especially supply chain finance, which, due to the blockchain real-time tracking of the goods, the payments, the contracts, hence improving the speed and eliminating the delay.

Example: Predefined conditions are automatically executed in the blockchain-based smart contracts, which eliminate intermediaries and incur less cost. For example, insurance payout can be released the moment the verification of claims is done.

Big Data Analytics: Empower Insights and Personalization

Big data analytics help financial institutions deal with massive amounts of data and allow them to arrive at actionable insights that benefit customer engagement and operational effectiveness.

- **Consumer Behaviour Analysis:** Spending habit trend can be analyzed to understand the trend and preference, thus helping financial institutions to provide products according to the needs of customers.
- **Credit Scoring:** Traditional models of credit scoring are based on very few touch points, whereas big data analytics considers diversified sources such as social media activity and mobile phone use to generate comprehensive profiles of creditworthiness.
- **Customized Products:** With each individual customer profile, banks can design tailored products, be it loan terms or investment products.

Example: Big data enables a bank to identify those customers that will be needing home loans by tracking their browsing and financial history and can thus contact them with offers in advance.

Mobile Technology: Democratizing Financial Inclusion

Low-cost smartphones and high-speed internet access have been a big boon in reaching financial services to the common people, particularly in underprivileged rural areas of the country. Mobile technology bridges the gap in the urban and rural population by easily facilitating access to banking, payment, and investment services through their own smartphones. For instance, farmers in villages can receive government subsidies directly into their mobile wallets.

- **Digital Payment:** Mobile phone-based UPI and QR Code-based payment systems gave speed and convenience, leaving cash with less bargaining power.
- **Financial Literacy:** Sometimes, tutorials and budgeting are integrated into mobile phones. It helps one learn better ways of management.

Example: A small business owner gets a mobile app that could empower them to digitally track all expenses, process their payments digitally, and apply for microloans electronically-all functions that would change how they run their business.

1.3.2 Revolutionizing Legacy Banking Models

The convergence of technologies really changed the traditional bank models. In fact, financial services have become more accessible, secure, and user-friendly. Customers do not have to visit their branches for basic services; instead, they are now performing transactions, investing, or accessing credit with a mouse click.

- **Efficiency Gains**: Automation powered by AI and big data reduces processing times and operational costs.
- **User's Experience** - The combination of blockchain and mobile technology combines reliability and convenience with secure and easy-to-perform transactions. Inclusiveness: Bringing millions into the world leads to a circle of economic inclusion through fintech products.

1.3.3 Consumer Behaviour

Changing Consumer-Modern consumers are shifting the dimensions of financial services to ones that require convenience, speed, and personalization. Since technology has become something indispensable in everyday life, so far, providers of financial services have been compelled to become more innovative and adapt to new expectations. Financial technology companies are at the forefront in leading this change; thus, it applies advanced tools in the development of solutions that address consumers' needs.

1. On-Demand Services: Immediate Access Anywhere, Anytime

Today, everything is surrounded by claims of instant financial services. This means there is no need to actually go to the branch or wait for the approval of such long periods of time. Transferring money, applications for loans, account balances, and many other things can be done within an instant with seamless communication.

- **Banking:** Online and mobile banking have enabled users to perform any transaction, pay bills, or manage investments from anywhere and at any time. Lending: Digital lending offers loan approval in an instant; it makes use of AI and Big Data to assess credit in a few minutes with absolutely no paperwork.
- **Payments:** Peer-to-peer payment services and mobile wallets enable money transfer in a split second-be it splitting bills in restaurants or sending money home to family members.

Example: A gig economy worker receives a microloan in minutes on a digital lending app and meets urgent cash needs, thus not making a trip to the bank.

1.3.4 Personalized Solutions: Tailored to User Preference

In their depth, personalization lies at the very core of new financial services offered through fintech firms, as they provide those tools and solutions that correspond to what users want and need.

- **Budgeting Applications:** Applications for budgeting, including Mint and YNAB, apply data analytics and create a deeper understanding of user-specific spending, hence setting better and tracking goals for your finances.
- **AI-driven Robo-Advisors**: AI-driven robo-advisors provide customized investment portfolios based on the financial objectives, risk tolerance, and income of the user. • Digital Wallets Mobile Wallets: Mobile wallets will provide recommendations to the user on discounts, cashback offers, and rewards by studying his transaction history. Example: A young professional gets saved for a house in five years through robo-advisor. He receives personalized recommendations from them. 3. Better Customer Experience Interface and Interaction Smarter and Seamless Interfaces
- A seamless user experience is one of the most critical things to fintech success, as today's consumers expect intuitive interfaces and innovative features that simplify financial interactions.
- **User-Friendly Interface:** Fintech apps are designed with minimalistic dashboards and clear navigation, making sure accessibility even for nontechnical users.
- **24/7: Chatbots and AI-powered virtual assistants** provide round-the-clock customer support to help users resolve queries or complete transactions at any time.
- **Voice-Activated Commands:** Users can perform activities like balance inquiries or the initiation of a payment with the help of emerging technologies such as voice recognition.

Example: A small business owner depends on a mobile banking application with voice-activated features to initiate fund transfers while multitasking, saving precious time.

1.3.5 The Push for Innovation: Fintech's Response to Consumer Demands

Increasing consumption and growth of consumers with ever-higher expectations have made fintech companies innovate and continuously develop in the environment of competition to exist. A few key approaches include:

Agility in Development: Fast iterative prototyping allows Fintech platforms to grow with customer needs at a speed akin to technologies that get developed.

- **Integration of New Technologies**: AI, blockchain, Big Data analytics are integrated into platforms to enhance features from both functionality and security perspectives.
- **Inclusiveness:** Solutions have to be inclusive-regional languages, voice guidance, features for people with low digital literacy.

1.3.6 Regulatory Support

All these were enabled by the governments and regulators across the world, and a lot has been owed by the regulators in really fostering the growth of the much-touted fintech segment. Regulators came forward with policies that facilitated the security of innovation and protected customers as well. Regulatory sandboxes provide access to evaluate and test innovative Fin-tech solutions in a special small-controlled environment that helps perfect and fine-tune such product standards.

- **Data Privacy Laws:** Regulations like the GDPR have made certain that personal data of consumers is kept safe, thus building trust in online financial platforms.
- **Financial Inclusion Programs:** National governments of India have adopted initiatives such as Pradhan Mantri Jan Dhan Yojana through which unbanked groups can be integrated into a financial system. Such efforts boosted the adoption of digital platforms for payments and mobile-based banking.

Innovation being regulated, the authorities have given a way forward and enabled an environment that has seen fintech grow while at the same time ensuring consumer protection.

1.3.6 Globalization

Fintech went global: borderless banking, cross-border payment systems turn out solutions to cross the geographical and currency barriers for businesses and people.

- **Cross-border payments**: inexpensive, real-time international transactions make life easier for small business owners and freelancers.
- **Global Financial Inclusion:** Fintech solutions serve as a bridge for including the underserved people in less developed nations into the wider world market through economic participatory inclusion.
- **Support for Multiple Currencies:** Again, the wallets, together with the payment gateways, have been able to support holding and transacting multiple currencies in order to reach the globe.

Globalisation has spread not only the wings of fintech companies but also wakened the need for cooperation between nations in building standard frameworks for digital finance.

1.4 CHALLENGES AND RISKS IN FINTECH

While Fintech has transformed the face of finance, this exponential growth is not without a number of challenges that have to be met if sustainable development and wide diffusion are to take place. Such potential downsides underline the complexity of integrating technology with financial services.

14.1 CYBERSECURITY THREATS

The increased use of digital platforms has thus brought growing cybersecurity concerns for fintech companies. Possible misuse of user data and finances opens up possibilities for cyber attacks, hacking, phishing scams, and data breaches.

- **Data Breaches:** Cyber attackers have the potential to steal customer information, including account numbers and personal details.

- **Fraudulent Activities:** Phishing scams and identity theft compromise account information, leading to financial losses for both the user and the service provider. • Infrastructure Vulnerabilities: Most fintech applications use cloud services and APIs quite aggressively, which, if left open, become vulnerabilities.

Example: Phishing of any digital payment platform can easily trick the user into divulging login credentials, thus resulting in unauthorized access. All this is possible only when fintech companies invest in proper encryption methods, real-time fraud detection systems, and cybersecurity awareness programs for users.

1.4.2 Regulatory Challenges

Fintech is an area where tremendous dynamism and innovation have taken place and, on many occasions, has outran regulatory capability. This created tension between innovation and compliance.

The negative impact of non-uniform regulations, whereby different countries and their respective regions come up with their own set of regulations, makes standardization tough to achieve for fintech companies.

- **Compliance Costs:** The stringent regulatory requirements, many times consuming in terms of time and resources for startups, may be overly costly.
- **Dynamic Policies:** The rapidly changing regulations may be deleterious to the long-term planning and investment by Fintech businesses.

Example: Cryptocurrency platforms are very uncertain about the regulatory scenario in most countries, including India, where governments are still in a spree to formulate policies on digital assets. It needs the right balance between innovation and regulation so that fin-tech growth does not get compromised on the altar of consumer protection.

1.4.3 Digital Divide

However, despite the wide proliferation of fintech solutions, not all socio-economic groups can access or be benefited from them. A kind of digital divide-a gap between those with and without access to digital tools-remains a major challenge.

- **Inadequate Infrastructure:** Access to the internet and smartphones has been poor in areas located far from the city center, which has adversely affected the adoption of fintech solutions.
- **Digital Literacy:** The target users, a significant proportion of them, cannot even read, let alone use any fintech applications and thus cannot be reached by any services.
- **Affordability:** While Fintech intends to cut costs, accessing smartphones and data packs will be unaffordable to low-income groups.

Example: Fintech platforms in India have thrown in initiatives such as regional language support and voice-guided apps to reach out to their non-English-speaking clients, but much more needs to be done to really scale up and bridge the digital divide.

1.4.4 Scalability Issues

Scaling operations is a common challenge for fintech startups, with the pressure being particularly strong when expanding into new markets or serving an increasingly large customer base.

- **Global Expansion**: Opening to the global market requires adherence to local regulations, cultural adjustments, and infrastructure investments.
- **Constraints on Infrastructure:** Such high growth puts pressure on old systems, which could eventually lead to degraded performance; this might be slower transaction speed or even system crashes.
- **Competition:** Competition in fintech is fierce, with more established players often far ahead in terms of resources and scale.

Example: A digital lending offering from a fintech startup may encounter problems in its international expansions due to variations in credit systems, behaviour of consumers and regulatory environments.

With such potential, it will surely revolutionize the financial industry, but for that, all these challenges have to be addressed in order for it to see long-term success: investment in cybersecurity, working with regulators on supportive policies, designing inclusive solutions that bridge the digital divide, and plan strategically for scalability. If such issues are handled proactively, then fintech can keep innovating while building trust and making the services accessible in every nook and corner of the world with due security.

1.5 COMPONENTS OF FINTECH ECOSYSTEM: INTERDEPENDENCE

The various elements constituting the fintech ecosystem create and provide financial services and oversight in concert with each other. Among startups, incumbent financial institutions, government regulators, and the consumer stand as interrelated building blocks; these are all among those on the front seats to take active participation regarding what will be the general outline in the landscape within the Fintech sector.

1.5.1 Startups: Solution Innovation at a Niche Level

Main players for innovation in this ecosystem are the fintech startups. These create solutions on specific niches, responding to gaps or inefficiencies within traditional financial services.

Function: FinTech participate in introducing innovations such as blockchain, AI, and mobile platforms to produce the kind of products like digital wallets, robo-advisors, and peer-to-peer lending sites.

Advantage: These innovations mainly replace traditional practices; instead, they make the practices quicker, less hectic, and expensive to afford.

- **Interface of Other Sub-units:**
- Inclusion of the solution in financial mainstream by Partner banks.
- Regulatory imperatives to keep in mind while innovating
- Need/push from the customer/Consumer to have financial services available on an Easy, Effective and Accessible.

Example: A fintech startup designs a mobile app that streamlines personal budgeting and expense tracking, catering to the pain point of millennial consumers.

2. Banks and Financial Institutions: Adopting or Collaborating with Fintech

The traditional banks and financial institutions remain one of the biggest players in the fintech ecosystem. They embrace changes brought about by technology to be relevant.

- Role: Banks adopt fintech solutions to achieve digitization, improved customer experience, and efficiency.
- Contribution to the Ecosystem: They bring established infrastructure, regulatory expertise, and trust that enables fintech solutions to scale.

Interaction with Other Components:

- Partner with startups for co-development innovative products or outright buying of solutions.
- Cooperate with regulators in ensuring that new technologies conform with financial laws.
- Engage customers by embedding fintech innovations into traditional offerings, including digital banking and instant payments.

Example: A bank may collaborate with any fintech company to introduce a UPI-based phone application and reach techno-savvy customers in the process.

3. Government and Regulators: Creating Enabling Frameworks

The governments and regulators have a very significant role in keeping the way in which the fintech functions within secure, ethical, and compliant dimensions.

- Role: They enact policies, rules, and regulations for consumer protection and financial stability.
- Contribution: Regulatory sandboxes allow fintech startups to do the testing of their innovations in a controlled environment, for instance. Data protection laws protect consumers against any potential misuses.
- **Interaction with Other Components:**
- Regulating banks and startups so that frauds and cyber attacks can be prevented.
- Infrastructure and incentives to adopting fintech by consumers through Digital India initiatives in India.

Example: A government issued a regulatory framework that allowed exchanges to operate well within legal parameters, allowing innovation with minimum risk.

4. Consumers: The Demand for Better Financial Services

Consumers are the backbone in the fintech ecosystem, whereby their needs and preferences create drivers of innovation and adoption.

- Role: Their demand for convenience, speed, and personalization compels the fintech companies and banks to create user-centric solutions.
- Contribution: Early adopters of fintech products provide the impetus that builds up the momentum for mass adoption and provides a direction toward which future innovations must head.
- **Interaction with Other Components:**
- Give something back to the startups by way of feedback, which would help them to refine their products.
- Adopt services provided by banks that incorporate fintech solutions.
- Benefit from government policies directed at making financial services more accessible and inclusive.

Example: Rural consumers are using digital wallets for transactions, and that's forcing fintech companies to develop solutions in regional languages.

Interdependence and Interaction Among Components

It evolves as a dynamic ecosystem where these elements affect and assist the rest:

1. **Startups and Banks:** The startups require the banks for their infrastructure and consumer trust, while the banks get an excellent chance to adapt the innovative inputs of the startups and upgrade their services accordingly.
2. **Start-up and Regulators:** It is the role of the regulatory bodies to ensure that they are in compliance with financial laws; conversely, start-ups bring in the knowledge that shapes progressive regulations.
3. **Banks and Consumers:** The fintech solutions being implemented by banks raise the experience for the customer; hence, banks satisfy particular needs which are in the demand list of the consumer.
4. **Regulators and Consumers:** Government policies encourage consumers to participate in financial services in a safe, accessible, and affordable manner.
5. Startups and Consumers: Direct contact with consumers would allow them to work out pain points and come up with some specific solutions.

Illustrative Example

A Fintech startup develops a peer-to-peer lending platform, directly connecting the borrowers and lenders.

- Startup: The platform offers a seamless user experience by deploying AI in creditworthiness assessment and matching of lenders and borrowers.
- Bank: Collaborates on the banking infrastructure to transfer funds.

- Regulators: Ensure the operations on the platform work within the set lending regulations and protect consumer interests.
- Consumers: Fast loan approvals for borrowers and higher returns compared to savings accounts for depositors.

This interdependence will be the root of innovation, confidence, and assurance that the fintech ecosystem moves and develops in service of the needs of all participants.

1.6 CAREER OPPORTUNITIES

The industry has experienced growth and inclusions in almost every aspect of the financial field, thus opening wide fields of opportunities within the Fintech sector.

Top Career Roles:

- Data Analysts and Scientists: Experts in deciphering financial data to yield better decision-making.
- Blockchain Developers: The professionals deal in building systems that are decentralized and also digital currencies.
- Financial Analysts: Experts in the art of dealing in the management of investment portfolios using AI-powered tools.
- Product Managers: They lead the product development and enhancement for a host of fintech products.

It helps in attaining financial inclusion, enhances economic efficiency, and supports the digital economy. In a world where digital connectivity propels global commerce, it is fintech that will help in frictionless transactions, access to credit, and innovative solutions for businesses and consumers alike.

Probably the most far-reaching influence of FinTech has to do with financial inclusion. It is a guarantee of easy access to financial inclusions at cheaper costs for people excluded from the traditional financing mechanism. Most people in most developing countries lack traditional banking either due to the lack of infrastructure or for geographic constraints. Fintech firms like M-Pesa have been able to fill this gap in places like Kenya using mobile-based payments services. Millions of people can now handle financial transactions with their mobile phones sans bank accounts. Equally, microfinance platforms such as Kiva allow individuals and small businesses to access microloans that will enable entrepreneurship and economic empowerment.

Fintech further streamlines the efficiency of the economy by automating financial processes and hastening service delivery at lowered costs. Automating regular activities for finance, such as payment and lending processing and customer services, reduces operation costs in financial institutions. The lending platforms powered by Fintech, for example, lower the cost of loan origination through the direct linking of borrowers to investors for loan origination processes without the traditional intermediary's interference-that is, the bank.

Other than that, fraud prevention and security are in focus, as the development of this arena of digital transactions increased the chances of cybercrime. Fintech, however, is the relief with the use of AI, machine learning, and blockchain. Real-time monitoring through an AI-powered detection system flags suspicious activities or prevents financial crimes. The blockchain guarantees data integrity and transparency; therefore, fraud or tampering with the financial records is very minimal. A very good example of this is Ripple's blockchain-based payment network, which allows financial institutions around the world to have secure cross-border payments.

It enables digital payments, e-commerce, and online marketplaces, all of which are necessary for the digital economy to function. PayPal, Stripe, and Square have changed how companies make payments; even SMEs today can reach most global trades. Online marketplaces such as Amazon and Shopify depend on fintech integrations that handle transactions, manage currency conversions, and offer customers options in how they pay across borders.

Example: Fintech is being utilized by the governments, too, in extending vital services to people. India's digital payment system linked with Aadhaar, direct benefit transfers, reduces corruption and makes sure that the fund disbursement actually reaches the beneficiaries efficiently. Several governments during the COVID-19 pandemic used fintech-powered platforms to distribute emergency relief funds in record speed, thus showing the scalability of service delivery through the use of the technology.

Fintech has grown in prominence as part of today's world economy by furthering financial inclusion, improving efficiency in operations, raising the bar on security, and ultimately enabling digital commerce. Applications transform industries in innovative ways that build toward a future of finance with technology-driven solutions that spur transparency, accessibility, and economic growth.

CHAPTER 2

DIGITAL TRANSFORMATION IN FINANCE

2.1 INTRODUCTION

With the digital transformation in finance, everything about the financial services, consumption, and delivery is changed. Integration of these technologies like AI, block chain, and big data has transformed this space to be agile and customer-centric and efficient space in finance's are provided, consumed, and administered has fundamentally changed with digital transformation in finance. With AI, block chain, and big data converging, the financial sector has transformed into agile, customer-centric, and efficient space. This chapter gives a snapshot of what digital transformation means in finance and how this might have implications for banking, payments, and the wider financial system. The examples come from India's rapidly changing digital landscape.

The replacement of old financial systems and methods by new technologies defines digital transformation in finance. Earlier, to deposit or withdraw money, a person would have to visit banks. Now, within minutes, this is possible on their mobile phone or computers. This makes the lives of people and companies easier, as they are no longer dependent on infrastructure to acquire access to finance.

Artificial intelligence is one of the most revolutionary technologies in finance. With artificial intelligence, financial institutions can analyze huge amounts of data related to customers, understanding behaviour and preferences as well as money-spending patterns. Banks and other fintech companies can then make services very personalized based on such analysis. For instance, an AI system could recommend savings plans or an investment strategy that matches someone's spending habits and long-term goals. Such personalized interactions not only give satisfaction to the customers but also build trust in digital banking services. Apart from personalization, AI plays a huge role in security enhancement. Its real-time monitoring of accounts can detect unusual transactions and may indicate fraud. For example, if a credit card is used for a high-value purchase in a foreign country with the cardholder still in India, the system flags this transaction and alerts the customer. With the recent rise of online transactions happening in India, AI and its ability to secure it has become indispensable in securing consumer confidence in digital finances.

Another game-changer in the financial sector is block chain technology. Serving as an immutable, secure digital ledger, block chain records every transaction transparently. A block chain entry once added cannot be modified or amended, hence perfect for most industries where the levels of security and accountability are really high.

This technology is highly impactful in areas such as crypto currency and cross-border payments. For instance, Indian companies dealing in international trade can use block chain for transactions securely and efficiently. Compared to traditional methods that mostly rely on high charges and a long processing period, block chain allows for an immediate transfer with low charges. This process cuts the cycle time by removing middlemen and further reduces fraud risks and data breaches. With the promise of simplifying trade finance and increasing transparency, block chain has emerged as a building block of digital transformation in India's financial ecosystem.

Big data is one of the primary drivers of digital transformation for financial institutions because it allows them to gather and analyze large volumes of information. This includes customer preferences, spending habits, and financial behaviours, which are essential to provide customized services. For example, it can help the banks of India analyze the credit history of the customer, and his or her income, to ascertain the eligibility to grant a loan. At the same time, while increasing the speed of a loan application, it enhances fairness and accuracy. Big data also helps financial institutions identify trends and predict market behavior, thereby enabling them to design innovative products and services. For instance, the bank can come up with special offers or cashback schemes based on spending patterns during festive seasons, which would boost the engagement and loyalty of their customers. In this regard, financial institutions can outperform the competition while ensuring that their customers' dynamic needs are met through big data.

The digital transformation in finance has seen tremendous impact in India, particularly through mobile wallets and Unified Payments Interface (UPI). These systems have changed the way people make payments. They are instant, convenient, and secure. For example, UPI allows users to link multiple bank accounts to a single mobile application, making it seamless to transfer funds with just a few clicks.

This will now even benefit the systems to remote places of the country. Farmers can directly get their money in mobile wallets for the produce grown from rural areas without any mediator. This saves time but reduces the cost of doing business. Digital payment systems also enhance transparency in financial activities, making it easier for the government to trace its economic activities and reduce corruption.

Digital transformation has also provided a global relevance to the financial ecosystem of India. With its booming tech industry and a large population using smartphones, India has emerged as the world leader in digital payment systems. The approach India has taken to integrate technology with finance has not only modernized its economy but has also made it an example for other developing nations.

Digital transformation in finance is highly relevant today than it's ever been. Technological advancement ensures that financial services are accessible to everyone: whether one lives in the city or in a remote area. Technology reduces the cost, enhances security measures, and provides personalized experience, making it a cornerstone for modern economic development. Indicative of this potential is India embracing these very technologies.

2.2 ROLE OF TECHNOLOGY IN BANKING

Technology has improved service delivery and enhanced operational efficiency and extended customer reach. Banking operations, such as depositing money, withdrawing cash, and even asking for a loan, used to require visits to physical bank branches. Currently, services like these are provided online and allow customers to conduct almost all their banking from a computer or a mobile phone. With technology, the way banks run their business has changed so much that it is quicker, more convenient, and more accessible to the customer, especially in distant places.

Among the most influential technological innovations that have shaped banking is the advent of Automated Teller Machines (ATMs). The ATMs. enable consumers to access banking services conveniently by withdrawing cash, depositing money, and checking on account balances at any convenient time without having to travel to a bank branch. This 24/7 accessibility has transformed banking and helped more customers to easily avail of basic financial transactions.

India is probably one of the most transformative ATMs. being used to provide financial inclusion. Such facilities are particularly crucial for rural and semi-urban localities where traditionally people have to travel a great distance to reach the nearest bank branch. Installation of ATMs. in these places has brought banking services to the doorsteps of the people, which allows them to carry out their banking operations without much disruption in their lives. For example, farmers can now withdraw money to buy seeds or pay laborers directly from the ATM located in their village.

Accessibility: The biometric-secured ATMs. have further enabled accessibility in India. For instance, instead of having to make use of PINs for verification, these machines allow a user to access his accounts using a fingerprint or an iris scan, thus extending services for all individuals irrespective of literacy levels or even comfort levels with traditional PIN-based authentications. Thus, this innovation has enabled the greater proportion of the population, especially the elderly and less-educated individuals, to access the formal financial systems.

ATMs. have also played a role in expanding the digital economy as it has supported cashless transactions. Most of the ATMs. now provide services like mobile recharge, utility bill payments, and mini statements, which minimizes the use of cash while providing customers with flexibility as needed. This multi-functionality is in line with India's push toward a less-cash economy as promoted by government initiatives like Digital India.

It also made available local employment through the provision of ATMs. in remote areas. People are engaged in the working of ATM kiosks, replenishing cash, and ensuring that customers can utilize those machines. This aspect is an economic addition to installing ATMs, because along with financial inclusion, community development is also provided with a boost.

Artificial Intelligence (AI) and Machine Learning (ML) are rapidly changing how banks operate or interact with their customers. AI-based system helps in the detection of anomalous transactions which might be the result of fraud. Such as a credit card getting used somewhere else while this person is still in India, and it will signal this and alert the respective customer. In a similar way, ML models analyze customer data to provide customized recommendations, such as saving plans or suitable loans according to the customers' spending habits. Automation has resulted in making banking operations precise and efficient. For example, loan applications that required manual review and documentation previously are now processed by automatic systems. It automatically evaluates the creditworthiness of a customer based on the customer's financial history and decides within minutes. In India, this has helped small businesses and individuals access credit, which helps boost economic growth.

In India, biometric-enabled ATMs. have made it easy for those who do not know how to write to do banking. Those ATMs. use either fingerprints or iris scans instead of using traditional PINs; this way, the customer can safely access their account. It is a great deal of change for the majority of the rural and aged people, who have found it hard to remember the passwords or manage the digital devices. For example, by using chatbots for customer service, one realizes how technology is making better experiences in banking by providing support instantly, which is dependable, user-friendly, and accessible. A chatbot is a computer program built on the AI system meant to handle the widest range of interactions with customers from simple inquiries and answers to answering more frequent queries, guiding a user through complex bank procedures. They are available 24 hours a day, seven days a week, providing the clients with instant help when they need it instead of wasting time waiting through more conventional customer care channels.

Chatbots are really helpful in dealing with repeated queries like balance in an account, transaction status, and even details about products offered by banks. By doing so, it relieves the human representative for more complex issues. They, therefore, enhance the efficiency of a customer service operation. As an example, a person who would like to be informed about how much more they qualify for as loans can simply go through the chatbot and calculate, in real-time, therefore, having the information handy and correct. In India, the chatbots were designed with the linguistic plurality of the country in consideration. Most banks have developed regional language-supporting chatbots, which allow most non-English-speaking customers to easily access the services of the bank. It is very essential in a country where most prefer communication in their mother tongue. For example, a farmer in a rural area may use a Hindi or Tamil chatbot to ask about crop insurance or account details, so that language barriers do not prevent access to financial services.

Chatbots also improve the customer experience by offering personalized interactions. By analyzing user data, they can provide tailored recommendations, such as suggesting savings plans or credit card options based on spending habits. This allows customers to appreciate themselves when they use the product so that they can have it easy trusting digital banking. Another thing is that an advanced AI chatbot does use natural language processing which makes it more conversational as it tries to figure out what a customer may be asking for hence doing things more humanly.

Another advantage of chatbots is that they can be used for troubleshooting. For example, if a customer has an issue with a failed transaction or needs assistance on how to use mobile banking services, the chatbot will be able to provide step-by-step instructions. Instant support solves problems and creates confidence in customers to use digital tools.

It also aligns with India's push toward digital inclusion and better customer service in banking. In the integration of regional language capabilities, real-time assistance, and personalized recommendations, chatbots have enabled banking access for hundreds of thousands of users. This streamlines the support system provided to customers further, driving how AI is transformative in terms of user-centric and inclusive financial services. Banking is opened to people who are not into the financial world due to technology. In India, mobile apps for banking are very common, enabling customers to send money, pay bills, and maintain accounts easily. Many of them support vernacular language as well, so anyone irrespective of their linguistic background can use them easily. There is no doubt that technology has revamped the banking scenario as it became more accessible, efficient, and customer-friendly. Innovations like AI, automation, and biometric systems brought the financial service to both urban and rural India at the doorstep of the poor by crossing regional borders of any Indian state. Therefore, further development of technology promises even better conditions and becomes more relevant to the changed world today.

2.3 DIGITAL PAYMENT SYSTEMS

Now, digital payment systems stand as the mainstays of the new-age economy, allowing for transactions in the absence of the usual physical cash. Using innovations like mobile wallets, online payment gateways, and contactless cards, the fast, convenient, and secure methods of making payment are offered by digital systems. It means that paying bills, transferring money, or shopping online can be done within seconds for individuals, whereas for businesses, this simplifies the process, ensures smooth operation, and provides easier processes like payroll, vendor payments, and other transactions.

One of the most significant features of a digital payment system is it can execute real-time transaction processing. Consider a case where a business needs to pay its employees on the same day; this digital payment system allows for just that by transferring funds instantly. These immediate payment services providers have been transformative for small businesses in India because they have allowed them to keep cash flow and operate their day-to-day activities with no delay. It is especially important for the modern economy where time is a resource. Transactions in these digital systems are secure due to advanced technologies, such as encryption and two-factor authentication (2FA). Encryption is the process of rendering sensitive financial information into coded form that can only be read by authorized users. Meanwhile, 2FA adds an extra layer to security by requiring users to verify their identity through some other method, such as a text message code or biometric scan. Thus, fraud and unauthorized access are prevented, making the digital payment safer than any cash handling. Near-Field Communication is the name of some innovations, further smoothing out the process of a payment. It provides payment from just tapping their card or mobile device on the terminal while making a payment in the store. NFC took good shape in India as more and more people were required to reduce contact during the pandemic Covid-19 time; however, the ease of transactions was given top preference in every routine purchases-including grocery shop-to-restaurants.

The Indian government also initiated massive efforts to encourage digital payments. Cashless transaction and digital wallet promotion programs were funded to incentivize consumers and companies to shift from cash to digital payment modes. Subsidies, pensions, and other government benefits were also directly credited into users' digital accounts, which made for a very efficient and transparent process. There has been a particularly significant impact in rural areas where access to financial services was limited.

Digital payment systems have also played a very important role in the emerging e-commerce sector of India. Online marketplaces heavily rely on such digital payment platforms to make the transaction between buyers and sellers simpler. These systems enable customers to pay through UPI, mobile wallet, and debit cards among others, thus making sure that they have a hassle-free shopping experience. Likewise, companies can reach the vast audience and make sure that they avoid cash-based transactions as much as possible.

Beyond convenience, the digital payment systems have contributed significantly to greater financial inclusion through entry into formal financial institutions for more individuals. Even rural India sees more people storing and transferring funds with mobile wallets after having been excluded from bank services prior. The language of their services provision will often be conducted in regional dialects ensuring greater access throughout the large populace.

The advancement of digital payment systems has not only made transactions swift and secure but also catalyzed India's move toward a more robust digital economy. Cashless payments and the enabler of small businesses are among the methods through which it enabled financial inclusion. Generally, it is important that one must have knowledge about these systems for undergraduate students because they will be shaping how money moves in the modern world

2.4 KEY INDUSTRY PLAYERS

A group of diverse stakeholders working together on the digital finance ecosystem transforms the approach in which financial services get delivered. Players include not only financial institutions and fintech startups but also some technology providers and regulatory bodies. Each player has made their unique contribution to achieve the dynamic and efficient development of a financial system; together, they have formed this ecosystem. The financial institutions include the most popular and well-known of the digital finance ecosystem players. Banks, in the earlier times, relied heavily on branches and physical presence, and the processes were completely manual for providing services. For depositing money or withdrawing funds, or just availing loans, people used to go to branches physically, which consumed precious time and was usually an inconvenient affair. But owing to digital tools, the functioning of banks has altered with a view to compete. They now offer internet banking and mobile apps from which their customers can handle their accounts anywhere, at any moment.

For instance, on internet banking, they perform various activities starting with electronic transfer of money up to bill payments, balance verification of accounts-activities now accessible from a comfort at home without needing a bank visit. With a cell app, additional functionalities become instant notifications of every transfer, insights about one's spending, voice command that helps them carry out similar functions. This change has had particular impact in India as banks work on trying to keep pace with a rapidly growing number of tech-savvy customers. With the incorporation of automated technologies like chatbots and AI-based support mechanisms, banks have improved their services to customers with immediate and timely resolutions.

Among the significant disruptors of this space have been fintech start-ups, which are companies that employ innovative technology to target niches like digital lending, investment management, and peer-to-peer payment systems. Product offerings from fintech start-ups are designed for younger consumers who value speed and convenience more than the traditional banks. For instance, online lending websites may offer loan applications and approvals in the shortest time possible, without any long-winding processes that may happen in traditional banking. Financial inclusion has been boosted among the underserved and in rural areas through fintech start-ups in India. Most people living in those areas are cut off from formal banking because of location or financial factors. The gap is covered by Fintech solutions that incorporate mobile wallets and micro-lending platforms, thereby allowing relatively affordable and accessible financial products to reach the households. Now, through the cell phone, farming families can acquire direct loans and payments for better tools and resources for their improvement of productivity. The collaboration between traditional banks and fintech start-ups has further enriched the digital finance ecosystem. Where traditional banks bring credibility as well as regulatory expertise to the table, fintech companies bring innovative technologies coupled with customer-focused solutions into the fray. In the case of hybrid services, both sectors are combined with the strengths of both combined to create services. As a result of such collaboration in India, integrated platforms have been developed where customers can access banking, investments, and payment services together.

This development indicates the evolving nature of the financial ecosystem, with innovation and inclusivity at the forefront. For undergraduate students, the interplay between traditional banks and fintech start-ups is valuable insight into the future of finance and the potential for technology to drive positive change in society.

Technology providers form the mainstay of the digital finance ecosystem. This supports the infrastructure tools and resources needed to ensure innovation. The providers support cloud computing services; with this, financial institutions find it possible to store the massive data volumes in a safe as well as efficient manner. It minimizes the need for costly physical infrastructure and makes the data accessible at any given time from anywhere. Technology providers also give companies data analytics tools to help them understand their customers better in terms of behaviour and preference. For example, financial institutions in India use data analytics to segment their customers into groups based on their spending habits and provide them with targeted financial products such as investment plans or credit cards tailored according to their needs.

Another revolution in the industry has occurred since the integration of AI on financial platforms through technology providers. Through AI, a bank or fintech startup can provide personalized services from investment advice based on certain goals or real-time systems for fraud detection during the transaction process.AI-based chatbots on banking platforms are common in India, helping customers get assistance in local languages within a few seconds. Innovations like these not only build customer experience but also trust in digital financial services.

This enables the regulators to ensure a proper system of the digital finance ecosystem in a safe, ethical, and transparent manner. Thus, these organizations make consumers aware of fraud and promote a stable financial system through proper guidelines. In India, regulatory initiatives such as Unified Payments Interface have revolutionized the payments landscape. UPI standardized digital payments, that is fast, secure and interoperable. This remains the leading initiative that makes many people adopt digital payment widely. This is as far as small businesses to individual users. Regulators set clear rules and allow innovation to give room for development of digital finance.

It is cooperation among stakeholders in driving the growth of financial services. For this reason, partnership between traditional banks and new fintech start-ups gives rise to the hybrid product, which can borrow both strengths, such as hybrid digital wallets connecting to bank accounts where the account holder can carry out any money management operations with much ease while leveraging the advantage of reliability and security found in traditional banking systems. Such cooperation have been very critical in meeting the varied needs of Indian residents, from sophisticated investing tools for urban professionals to simple payment solutions for rural users. With the help of a combination of government policy, technology, and customer demand, India has reached the top position in the global digital finance rankings. It would provide a strong foundation to support a robust digital ecosystem because of internet connectivity, increased digital literacy, and enhanced financial inclusion. Paradoxically, the agility of fintech start-ups as well as the technological skills of providers have provided space to create innovative solutions which cover a wide range of needs in finance. As a result, it becomes the benchmark for other countries in wanting to integrate technology in their financial systems. It has succeeded in its digital financial ecosystem because of each of its stakeholders' distinct contributions. Credibility and scale come from financial institutions; start-ups foster innovation and agility; technology businesses supply sophisticated tools and infrastructure; and regulators provide safety and trust.

These stakeholders of the Indian economy have, therefore, created a vibrant, inclusive financial system that empowers businesses and individuals alike. Understanding the roles and interactions of such players is very important for undergraduate students, as they gain valuable insights into how technology changes the financial world and drives sustainable economic growth.

2.5 BENEFITS OF DIGITAL TRANSFORMATION IN FINANCE

2.5.1 Better Customer Experience

The digital revolution has changed the way customers relate to finance services, and it incorporates both customized and convenient service. Mobile applications have led to users having a full view of their financial lives through apps, which may show them their balance or account activities and even bring them tailored advice on either saving or investing.. For instance, an app may suggest to a consumer who spends too much money eating out how much he ought to reduce using the usage patterns of spending. More than that, India's digital payments incorporated multiple languages of the country for ease of translation and access in this country with many linguistically diverse users, that creates value and an aspect of trust that adds more to the overall banking experience for customers.

These improvements are of great importance in countries such as India, where the expectations of consumers vary due to differences in financial literacy and usage of technology. For instance, a farmer in a rural area can use simple mobile banking applications to receive payment for his crops, track financial activities, and apply for loans without having to visit a bank office. The confluence of technology and user-centric design has made financial services more accessible and efficient for millions.

2.5.2 Operational Efficiency

It brought in a new dimension of efficiency in financial institutions through automation that has eradicated all the manual processes. In its wake, what could earlier take several hours or even days to accomplish-the approval of loans, or reconciling transactions-is done within a matter of minutes due to automation. For example, artificial intelligence (AI)-powered credit scoring models analyze an applicant's history and behaviour to give a credit score. This process not only hastens the approval of loans but also minimizes mistakes, and the process is fair and transparent. The above is transformatory for SMEs in India, which would always find it challenging accessing credits within a timely manner. Almost instantly, automated systems would evaluate loan applications. As a result, it gives business owners access to funds that allow them to grow and operate effectively. Automation further lowers the operational costs of financial institutions by freeing up resources in investing in strategic areas like how customers are served and how new innovative financial products can be developed.

Beyond lending, automation has simplified routine banking operations such as account monitoring and compliance reporting. For example, fraud detection systems scan transactions in real-time and flag suspicious activities that are detected in advance of being executed. The money risk of losing is much smaller, and these efficiencies-again, with India as one of the most rapidly digitizing countries for finance-banks and fintech companies have room to scale their service offerings while still delivering strong degrees of accuracy and security.

2.5.3 Financial Inclusion

Digital transformation has been that game-changer in bridging the gap that exists between the underserved people and formal financial services. Through mobile banking apps or even digital wallets, people living in rural areas where they do not have access to formal bank branches can perform all their essential financial activities from mobile phones. This, therefore, means that money can safely be stored, sent to one's family member, or accessed to get a small loan without visiting a formal bank. This has been particularly transformative in India, where large portions of the population are living in remote areas.

The government initiatives that can be considered as part of financial inclusion are promoting UPI. UPI facilitates instant and real-time transfer from one bank account to another even for those who have little technological know-how. Farmers can sell their produce to buyers in the city, and they can get their money directly into digital wallets. No middlemen are required; that way, farmers will get a fair price, fewer delays or risks associated with cash transactions. It brought changes in an individual's lifestyle but at the same time it built more resilient rural economies through incorporating a more integrated financial system.

Financial inclusion is more of empowerment rather than access only. The rural women had no say on the funds, and the digital platform has given them the option of self-governance while deciding and executing any monetary decision. Further to this transformation, digital literacy programs conducted in regional languages, further support the cause of educating people to use the platforms efficiently. Such efforts are very crucial for widespread financial empowerment in a country like India where diversity and regional disparities are pronounced.

2.5.4 Economic Transparency

The new era of digital payments has brought about a degree of transparency which was absent in the cash-based economies. Every digital transaction leaves a verifiable record, creating a financial trail that can be monitored and audited by regulatory authorities. Such transparency reduces the prevalence of activities like tax evasion, which are more difficult to identify in cash-based systems. The advent of digital payment systems in India has greatly facilitated the monitoring of economic activity and helped revenues be reported more accurately by the government. DBT is probably one of the best examples of economic transparency in action. Subsidies, pensions, and welfare payments are now directly deposited into beneficiaries' bank accounts, reducing leakage and ensuring that funds reach the intended recipients. This saves money for the government but increases public trust in its financial systems. Digital transparency makes businesses more accountable. Companies incorporating digital payment systems can very easily monitor their sales and expenses and profits. This reduces their chances of making errors that may lead to tax implications. It creates an open economic playing field where, on a fairer level of operation, businesses can trade. For people, the transparency in digital payments brings confidence in the financial system. The security and traceability of transactions make more people choose digital finance. Eventually, this gives a strong and accountable economy. So, in a country like India where transition from cash to digital payment has been rapid, such benefits emphasize the necessity for further investment in digital finance infrastructure and education.

2.5.5 Secure Transactions

Digital transformation has greatly improved the security level of financial transactions, with some of the risks that always characterize traditional methods being lessened. The Advanced encryption technologies ensure that any form of sensitive information, whether it is an account number and personal details, transforms into secure codes that one cannot easily access with regard to unauthorized users. That makes the online and mobile banking transaction much safer for the use of its users.

Apart from encryption, fingerprint scans, facial recognition, and iris scanning are increasingly being used in the Indian digital financial ecosystem to authenticate identities. The forms of identification make the identity of each user unique and non-duplicable and only allow authenticated users to access accounts or approve transactions. For example, the mobile banking apps in India often have biometric logins, which enhance security but are also convenient for users who might otherwise forget complex passwords.

AI-powered fraud detection systems enhance digital transaction security further. Such systems scan for patterns and alert suspicious activities in real time. For instance, should a credit card be applied in an unusual location or for a high-value transaction, the system will promptly alert the user and ensure that the transaction is put on hold until verified. This way, the users are more confident and reduction of losses from fraud cases happens. This makes the transactions online in India strictly apply two-factor authentication (2FA). It is now accepted as a standard norm requiring two different forms of proof of identity, including two different types of security-verifying elements, namely: a password and OTP as sent to the customer through his mobile phone; completing the transaction. With these high-tech measures, it has led more people to look at digital finance, which consequently has resulted in the evolution of a more sophisticated digital economy.

These developments in secure transactions are of great significance to a country like India, which is witnessing a pace that has never been witnessed in its transition from cash-based to digital payments. The financial institutions and the fintech companies, keeping the security aspect in consideration, help instill confidence among the users, thereby encouraging more people and businesses to join the digital financial ecosystem. In the long term, increasing security will be an indispensable factor in maintaining the trend of growth in digital finance in India. The benefits of digital transformation go way beyond the convenience factor-the digital transformation is changing everything from how one interacts with their financial services to how he/she does business. Advanced technologies enable financial institutions to not only enhance the customer experience and provide financial inclusion but also guarantee economic transparency. This cornerstone is secure transactions, which will instill the confidence and safety required for widespread adoption.

The phenomenal impact that digitalization had on the economy of India, mainly when it pushed millions of its citizens from the informal sector and finally started bringing these divergently positioned urban and rural economies closer. Remote individuals will have the potential to be in a financial ecosystem while never going to the branch of an actual bank; small companies, too, are likely to avail quick efficient payment. These innovations have also made India a worldwide leader in digital economy and an example for many developing countries. For the students, this understanding through the digital transformation in finance comes out as an area that has shaped the future and technology. It portrays how innovation can be brought about to solve real-time problems for economic growth while providing an inclusive financial system. Lessons learned from this India experience will be imperative as the digital landscape keeps unfolding over the years ahead to make it safe, efficient, and equitable.

2.5 CHALLENGES OF DIGITAL TRANSFORMATION

2.5.1 Cyber security Risks

With increased reliance on digital platforms by financial services, cyberattacks and data breaches have emerged as a much larger threat. Hackers are specifically interested in personal information, transaction records, and authentication credentials for their nefarious activities and represent a significant threat not only to consumers but also to institutions. For instance, phishing scams in which attackers trick users into divulging personal information by using a fake email or website have become a serious problem. Similarly, malware attacks can hack into an entire system, steal data or lock users out of their accounts until a ransom is paid.

This is precisely why the rapid growth of digital payment systems, like mobile wallets and Unified Payments Interface (UPI), underlines the critical need for cybersecurity in India. In a country where more and more people are resorting to digital platforms, the number of financial transactions carried out online has increased manifold and thus become an attractive target for cybercriminals. The only way financial institutions can be secure against these threats is to adopt the latest security measures, including end-to-end encryption, which secures data while in transit, and multi-factor authentication, which verifies a user beyond simple credentials.

It watches for patterns of transactions in real-time and can recognize suspicious transactions before the scam occurs. Artificial intelligence-based fraud detection systems also play an increasingly important role. Technology is critical, but equally important is teaching users to use the web properly and to avoid using weak passwords or opening suspicious links. An effective approach would be integrating technological advances with user awareness to manage cyber security risks as part of India's fast-developing digital economy.

2.5.2 Regulatory Compliance

This regulatory landscape is such a huge challenge for financial organizations because the rules on digital finance are so different in most regions and countries. Hence, this becomes a burden to international organizations because in this jurisdiction, the set of rules is made here to safeguard the consumer or prevent money laundering among various financial crimes and ensure all-round stability of the monetary system. This regulation would then be a resource intensifying process since the expenditure on legal expertise, the compliance technology, and continuous audits becomes necessary.

In India, the Reserve Bank of India (RBI) has brought in strict guidelines to govern the digital finance ecosystem. For example, measures to enforce Know Your Customer (KYC) norms ensure that all financial transactions are traceable, thereby reducing the risk of fraud and money laundering. Similarly, regulations on data protection mandate that institutions safeguard user information, aligning with global standards.

The dynamic nature of these regulations poses additional challenges. As technology evolves, new risks emerge, requiring regulators to update their guidelines frequently. For banks and fintech companies, this means constantly adapting their operations to stay compliant while maintaining their competitive edge. Balancing innovation with regulatory requirements is essential, as non-compliance can result in heavy penalties and loss of consumer trust.

Coordination of the regulators with other industry players is the essence for developing a sound and fair financial system. In India, through the innovation of regulatory sandboxes, fintech companies are empowered to experiment with innovative solutions while being in the watchful eyes of the regulators to ensure such solutions meet standards of compliance before going into the market. This enables innovations in keeping the environment secure for users.

The greatest challenge in the digital finance landscape remains cybersecurity risks and regulatory compliance. Investment in advanced technologies, fostering user awareness, and open communication with regulators are some of the strategies through which financial institutions can overcome these hurdles and create a secure, trustworthy, and innovative financial ecosystem.

2.5.3 Technology Adoption

Awareness and education are key barriers that impede the widespread use of digital financial tools. For instance, most people living in rural areas or not well educated are ignorant about the various functionalities offered by mobile wallets, online banking platforms, and digital payment systems. In this respect, a gap in knowledge of these applications is the significant barrier that prevents this huge section of people from being part of such advancements. In India, efforts to prevent this involved introducing digital literacy programs through which people would be sensitized on the use of digital financial tools. Such programs usually take the form of workshops in rural areas, where trainers show people how to download apps, do basic transactions, and secure their accounts with strong passwords. For example, community centers in villages can design programs that teach farmers how they can directly receive payments from buyers for their crops through mobile wallets. Initiatives like this have been not only instrumental in boosting participation in the digital economy but also empower persons in having control over their finances.

However, these efforts require continuance and scaling up to cater to a greater population. Added complexity comes from the difficulty of language barriers and skepticism against newer technologies and distrust of digital systems. Culturally sensitive approaches through the example of carrying tutorials in regional languages help boost the confidence levels of the users. With the increasing integration of digital financial tools into daily life, education is now an important step toward making access more equal.

2.5.4 Infrastructure Gaps

The bedrock of digital finance initiatives is reliable internet and mobile network access, but in India, there are many remote and rural areas where this is inadequate. These people cannot access mobile banking apps, make online payments, or complete digital transactions due to the lack of connectivity. The digital divide is limiting the reach of financial services most adversely affecting the communities that stand to benefit the most from digital inclusion.

Even the simple financial transactions such as checking account balances or even obtaining state subsidies digitally is very challenging in areas of poor network coverage in villages. For example, digital wallet payments from the sales of their produce by farmers will have to wait for a day or two due to poor network connectivity and that will disrupt financial planning. It calls for huge investments in telecommunication infrastructures to bridge the gaps.

Therefore, government policies on the issue of digital inclusion are the direct necessity for it. Under the Digital India campaign, the flagship programs have broadened high-speed broadband connectivity in many rural and far-flung regions in India. Similarly, affordably priced mobile handsets or smartphones along with tie-ups with the telecom operators at economical data plans have paved the way to accessing digital solutions. All these developments together ensure that the most depressed regions do not fall back from this much-needed digital change by having local-level awareness camps.

The gaps in infrastructure would have to be bridged through public as well as private partnerships in collaboration with telecom firms and fintech companies and between the latter and policy-making. It is through effective deployment of resources that identified areas may be served. People could then be empowered, making them capable of stimulating much more growth.

2.5.5 Resistance to Change

Digital transformation is also subjected to change. People and organizations have some hesitation to leave behind the way of doing things that has been traditional to them for many years and embracing the new digital way of life. The people have grown into accustomed ways, like conducting their transactions using cash or approaching a physical bank for every service. Most elderly individuals find digital tools scaring or redundant since they are grown using conventional ways. Another discouraging feature toward adoption would be that most people are mistrusting the digital system, being in the security of fear or lacking proper knowledge about it.

Cultural factors are the greatest influencers of attitudes toward digital finance in India. For example, cash remains the most preferred mode of payment within many communities due to the cultural value of cash, because it represents trust and control. Cultural affinity toward tangible transactions makes people resistant to making a switch toward intangible digital payments. Small, local businesses are likely not to embrace the solutions since they think the solutions would be too complicated or expensive to implement. Building consumer confidence would be the first step toward overcoming such resistance. That can be acquired through transparent communication where they explain how digital tools are actually working and the means taken to ensure security. That aside, simplification in platforms is also important; users should not need to worry about technical knowledge to maneuver around digital tools. This approach in India has helped make digital finance more accessible, particularly due to mobile banking applications and regional language-based payment platforms. Another key influencer to overcome resistance is consistent customer support. The way reliability in getting help-in the form of call center operations, in-person desks, even AI-driven chatbots-assures customers that help will be there when they need it while switching to digital service use boosts the rate of adoption. Campaigns where bank officials go door-to-door in rural regions and introduce digital services plus allay fears have boosted rates of adoption. These measures must be consistent enough to retain the users on the roll and ensure that they will continue to use digital banking services.

Even though adoption of digital banking has made consumer experience, financial access, and sector productivity significantly better, it is facing many challenges. Some of the major challenges are cybersecurity, accurate regulatory compliance, adaptation to the latest technologies, deficiency of infrastructure, and resistance to change. It has to overcome all of these to achieve long-term success.

These are even more crucial in India because of diversity of population and the differential level of digital literacy.However, there is little by little bearing fruit about enhancing digital literacy, upgrading regulatory frameworks, and further expanding connectivity. Initiatives by the government like Digital India are filling the infrastructural gaps as well as the educational gaps. Fintech innovations have also been able to simplify complex digital tools, thus rendering them accessible to everyone in a more inclusive and efficient financial ecosystem where people will feel confident in their approach towards digital finance.

2.6 CONCLUSION

There have indeed been very significant shifts pertaining to the delivery and experiences in financial services with regards to digital transformation. Digital transformation makes a system far easier for the users and rather more efficient for consumption purposes. For example, innovative efforts through mobile banking, systems for digital payments, as well as artificial intelligence applications have made this highly feasible. In India, then, through offered services from various financial sectors, its ability to transform and break away certain economic divides between those with and without is apparent.

One of the most important impacts of digital transformation is making people financially included. This means that most of the basic banking services were unaccessed by the people in those rural areas where physical banking facilities were not available. All that has changed with digital banking apps and wallets, since the people of the very remotest area can not only save money but also do transfer and avail credit on digital platforms. This has been enabling individuals to enter the formal economy and, in turn, promote India's overall economic growth.

Efficiency is yet another huge benefit of finance's digital transformation. Systems are now automated, making the processes of loan approval, transferring funds, and clearing bills quicker and more effort-free. This means businesses face less operational delay and find more channels for growth. In fact, SMEs in India have been on the receiving end of all these technologies, which have helped them access financial resources and operate their businesses effectively.

The adoption of digital finance solutions has thus spurred economic growth through increased innovation and entrepreneurship. Various start-ups in India came up with new financial products and services on the digital platform that cater to various customers. From investment tools to the lending platforms among peers, the innovations thus created the much-needed competition and a higher quality of financial service in both the local and global arenas.

Despite the challenges, India's success in implementing digital finance solutions has been an example for other developing nations. Government initiatives in the form of digital payments, such as the Unified Payments Interface (UPI), have set a global benchmark on how technology can be used to enhance financial ecosystems. These efforts have not only improved transparency and security in financial transactions but have also boosted public trust in digital systems. With continuous development of technology and infrastructure, the future of digital finance is much brighter in the coming days. With blockchains, artificial intelligence, and 5G connectivity, financial services will be secure, personalized, and accessible for all. India is emphasizing digital literacy and connectivity in its rural areas so that nobody is left behind in this transformation.

Therefore, with regard to the digital transformation in finance, it has redefined the industry as more inclusive, efficient, and innovative. The rapid progress of the nation in adopting these technologies also highlights the potential for global digital finance to drive economic growth and social progress. Undergraduate students would find this insight into the future of finance and its role in a better connected and equitable world enlightening.

CHAPTER 3

FINANCIAL MARKETS AND INSTRUMENTS

3.1 INTRODUCTION

Financial markets and instruments constitute the bedrock of all modern economies. They come in as channels through which people, businesses, as well as governments raise the much-needed capital, conserve money, and hedge some of the financial risks which may emerge. Financial markets are therefore critical to the economic growth of a country, employment, and distribution of wealth since they open avenues for saving exchange with required financing. Such markets pool together a vast array of participants, such as retail investors, institutional investors, regulators, and intermediaries, to work towards the maintenance of a dynamic and efficient financial ecosystem.

There are basically two types of financial markets, namely, capital markets and money markets. Capital markets deal with long-term investment tools such as stocks and bonds in order to help corporations to finance expansion and innovation. Money markets, on the other hand, deal with short-term financial instruments such as treasury bills and commercial papers that are meant to provide liquidity and stability in the financial system. These markets collectively constitute the backbone of an economy by ensuring that capital is distributed efficiently and effectively. The financial instruments used in these markets to carry out transactions are stocks, bonds, mutual funds, and derivatives. Each of the instruments is useful for various risk appetites and financial goals. For instance, stocks are equities that represent ownership in a company with the possibility of earning significant returns at higher levels of risk. Conversely, bonds provide an assured flow of income and are, therefore, liked by conservative investors. Mutual funds and exchange-traded funds pool the resources from many investors and create diversified portfolios to minimize risk while maximizing return. The knowledge of these instruments will help individual investors to take more informed decisions pertaining to their investments. The financial sector and its instruments have undergone huge transformation over the last years in India because of strong economic reforms, improved techno-support, and more and more retail investor participation. Bodies like SEBI improve the level of transparency among the financial market with all kinds of protection that develops the confidence level among individuals within the system. The advent of digital platforms has further democratized access to financial markets whereby people from all walks of life can participate and avail themselves of wealth creation opportunities. SIPs and other efforts of awareness campaigns have therefore been instrumental in the cause of promoting financial literacy and inclusion in the country. The undergraduate student learns more than an academic exercise of understanding financial markets and instruments; it becomes a practical necessity. It provides one with very crucial insights into the working of economies and helps in making better personal financial decisions. Even when the nation emerges as a globally growing superpower, finance knowledge in financial markets is bound to help students stay abreast of the happenings of the financial world. In case they elect to invest, or aspire to take up a lucrative career in finance, or want to contribute to a better policy-making, that would come about from effective understanding and application of basic concepts and principles

3.2 STOCK MARKETS AND TRADING PLATFORMS

Stock markets are the heartbeats of world economies. A stock market is an outlet where companies can issue their shares for raising funds to grow and expand. Those who purchase these shares in return become part owners of that firm. The process works effectively for both parties because through this method, the necessary capital will be acquired to grow and expand, whereas investors earn returns according to the good or bad performance of the company. The price of shares in a firm is determined by the market and depends on several factors, for example, how well the company is performing, investors' confidence, and broad economic trends. India's financial ecosystem majorly depends on two of the biggest stock exchanges in the country: Bombay Stock Exchange and National Stock Exchange. One of the oldest stock exchanges in Asia, the Bombay Stock Exchange was started as far back as 1875, and it is majorly responsible for governing the Indian equities market.

The NSE, on its part, is known to introduce electronic trading in India, making stock trading much faster and efficient. These transactions provide a controlled space to allow buyers and sellers share the same stock transparently and safely.

The use of technology has transformed the way people trade on the platforms of the stock markets. Olden days, the investors used physical exchange and brokers to place buy or sell orders. Now, one can trade from a smartphone or a computer. There are facilities like real-time stock prices, advanced analytics, and customizable dashboards. In India, it has become so easy to even the retail investor due to the number of apps that exist, such as Zerodha, Upstox, and many more. Such apps are offering educative material and very friendly interfaces so that one could begin easy.

The stock market is also the reflection of a country's economic health. High stock prices often denote that businesses are doing well, and the economy is on the upswing. Low stock prices may, however, point to challenges of the economy. For example, the COVID-19 pandemic witnessed very volatile markets across the globe due to the reaction of investors toward uncertainties. The markets recovered very strongly in India even after witnessing declines initially. It, therefore, points to the strength of the Indian economy and its ability to adapt to changing times. Investment in the stock market is fairly elementary, but people must know how it works. In India, exchanges and regulators have managed to educate individuals through initiatives such as Investor Awareness Programs about the benefits and risks of investing. These programs attract the participation of more people toward equity markets and financial inclusion and wealth creation. Thus, for an undergraduate, understanding the stock market is a wonderful skill that helps in providing financial literacy along with enabling long-term investment and also personal financial growth.

This way, the stock market and trading platforms form one of the significant elements of today's finance. It bridges the gap between businesses seeking capital and investors seeking growth opportunities. Growth in digital trading platforms has democratized access to Indian stock markets, which are now open to investment from people from all walks of life who want to build wealth. This enables students to understand how these markets operate and, as a consequence, take the first steps towards a lucrative profession in finance.

3.2.1 Case Study: A Successful IPO in India.

A new Indian consumer technology business has just recently launched its initial public offering, which received immense interest from both retail and institutional investors. It was looking to raise funds to finance the expansion, which would further support the development of new lines of products and upgrade its digital infrastructure.. The IPO went several times over-subscribed, which reflected high levels of investor confidence in growth potential and market position the company had.

The company priced its shares strategically in a manner that it remained affordable for the retail investor and yet did not sacrifice attractive valuations for the institutional participants. On listing, the stock started trading with a significant premium to the issue price, thus giving early investors spectacular returns. The result also demonstrated a rising interest among Indian investors in technology-driven firms.This IPO success underlines the importance of thorough planning, transparent communication, and market timing. For students studying financial markets, it provides a clear example of how companies can leverage the stock market to achieve strategic goals while offering investment opportunities to the public. It emphasizes the dynamic relationship between businesses and capital markets, which helps in understanding more about their impact on economic growth and wealth creation.3.3 Bonds and Mutual Funds

3.2.1 Bonds

A bond is a type of debt security that allows corporations, municipalities, and governments to raise capital by borrowing money from investors. When you buy a bond, you are essentially lending funds to the issuer in return for periodic interest payments, which are usually called coupon payments. At the end of the bond's term, or maturity, it is the issuer who shall return the face value to the investor. The income stream thus derived is predictable; hence, bonds are said to be an attractive investment opportunity for those seeking a stable and reliable return.

Bonds are said to be less risky compared to stocks as one receives fixed returns over an identified period. However, bonds are not risk-free. Interest rate risk is when changes in interest rates impact the market value of bonds. In an example, when the interest rate increases, the existing coupons with low rates are unattractive; therefore, the price for those decreases. Credit risk arises where the issuer has the probability of defaulting on payment of interest or principal to an entity issuing corporate bonds. There is a need to learn about such risks so as to take wise decisions towards portfolios by investors.

The most common issuers of bonds in India are the government and public sector companies. G-Secs are the popular names given to government bonds, and it is one of the safest investment avenues because the sovereign guarantee of the government stands behind them. These are apt for risk-averse investors who emphasize capital protection and steady income. Government bonds also provide one of the primary sources of financing to be used in the execution of public infrastructure projects including road construction, hospitals and school constructions, among many others, and therefore develop the country.

Corporate bonds are issued by private and public companies and offer higher yields compared to government bonds but bear a slightly higher risk. Corporate bonds are attractive to investors who want better returns while willing to take a moderate level of risk. Companies use the proceeds from corporate bonds for several purposes, such as expansion of operations, refinancing debt, or launching new products. Investors assess the creditworthiness of these companies using ratings provided by credit agencies, which would give an idea of the possibility of timely repayment.

The Indian bond market has high diversification and high accessibility to various investors-ranging from small savers to large institutions. More retail participation in bonds takes place with the availability of platforms that enable small investors to buy bonds directly. The RBI has also introduced initiatives, such as the Retail Direct Scheme, through which online portals enable direct investment into government bonds by retail investors, making bonds an all-inclusive financial instrument.

For the ones who seek to balance their portfolios, bonds are a very good option for risk diversification and the generation of stable income. During times of unstable economics, bonds can serve as a hedge against risks associated with uncertainty in the market, which can enable investors to meet their financial objectives with greater confidence. As part of the financial ecosystem, bonds not only help create personal wealth but also aid in the stability of the economy of the country at large.

3.2.2 Investment in Mutual Funds

Investment in mutual funds forms when a pool of money raised from different investors is managed to create a diversified investment portfolio in equities, bonds, and other securities, whereby the risks are reduced to a considerable extent as each investment is spread across varied types of assets and varied industries. For example, a laggard stock in the portfolio of a mutual fund may be cushioned off by better-performing securities so that the overall portfolio is relatively stable. Thus, mutual funds are always preferred by investors who seek a perfect blend of risk and return.

Mutual funds have become popular in India due to their accessibility and professional management. Skilled fund managers manage those funds, utilizing market expertise to maximize returns for investors while being in alignment with specific investment objectives. They cater to a wide range of financial goals and risk appetites through different options, such as:

- Equity Funds: These funds are stock-oriented and best suited for investors seeking long-term returns. Equity funds tend to carry higher risks because they are directly correlated with market performance.
- Debt Funds: These funds are bond-oriented and fixed-income securities, best suited for conservative investors who seek stability and regular income.
- Hybrid Funds: These funds have a hybrid mix of equity and debt, offering a balanced appeal for those seeking moderate risks and consistent returns.

The major attractive feature of mutual funds in India is the Systematic Investment Plans. SIPs provide for an investor to invest a fixed amount periodically, it may be monthly, quarterly, or yearly. This will be more comfortable for the individual with limited savings for investment in the market. This approach towards disciplined investment makes a habit of managing one's finances and brings rupee cost averaging in action so that the volatility would work out less with the duration of time.

Mutual funds also offer liquidity to investors who can sell units any time except with closed-end funds. Furthermore, people who do not like the thought of tying up their money often appreciate this ability to draw down on it when needed. The transparencies of mutual funds include portfolio composition disclosures, fees, and regular performance data, which builds investor confidence.

In India, mutual funds are regulated by the Securities and Exchange Board of India (SEBI). It ensures that mutual funds function in a transparent manner, in the best interest of the investor. SEBI has been enforcing on fund houses to provide all necessary details so that the investors make proper decisions. Public awareness programs like "Mutual Funds Sahi Hai" have also helped in educating the people about the advantages of mutual fund investments.

The growth of mutual funds in India reflects their ability to bridge the gap between professional financial management and individual investing. For undergraduate students and first-time investors, understanding mutual funds is a vital step toward financial literacy and long-term wealth creation. Through enabling participation in diverse markets with expert guidance, mutual funds make it possible to build financial security and achieve life goals.

BENEFITS AND RISKS

Both bonds and mutual funds provide their own set of advantages and disadvantages, best suited to various types of investors and financial goals.

Bonds: Bonds are one of the best options for conservative investors. They always want stability and predictable return. The income stream which is steady and predictable is an attractive feature for coupon payments to individuals who want regular cash flow, such as retirees. Moreover, bonds issued by the government are a low-risk investment because sovereign guarantees back them up. Therefore, it is a safe investment to save capital.

There are also risks involved with bonds: interest rate risk is experienced when market interest rates change which affects the value of already existing bonds. For example, if interest rates become higher, the prices of previously issued bonds tend to decline as newer bonds with higher yields are more attractive. A credit risk is also considered, especially for corporate bonds, as the issuer would fail to pay when his financial condition worsens. These kinds of risks need to be considered prior to the inclusion of bonds in their portfolio.

Mutual Funds: Diversification and professional management also provide mutual funds as a medium through which investors can make extra income. Most investors bring in their funds to invest together in forming a portfolio which then goes on to invest in several types of investments. This nature of diversification makes mutual funds very appealing to people who balance both risk and reward.

One of the significant advantages of mutual funds is the presence of professional fund managers, using their expertise to control market conditions and maximize your returns from your portfolio. Another reason mutual funds prove to be helpful is the flexibility they offer in choices such as Systematic Investment Plans wherein it is possible to invest small amounts periodically over a period of time.

Mutual funds do face market risks, as their value can change with changes in the economy and prevailing market trends. Investors are bound to lose if the market performs poorly. Some mutual funds also charge management fees and an exit load that could reduce returns by a few percentage points. One should therefore be aware of these costs and align them with their financial goals to maximize mutual fund investments.

In conclusion, bonds and mutual funds suit different profiles and objectives of the investors. Bonds are ideal for people who require stability and predictable income. Mutual funds are ideal for growth through diversification and expert management. Knowledge of benefits and risks will allow investors to craft a balanced portfolio aligned with their risk tolerance and long-term goals.

CASE STUDY: BONDS

Public sector organization in India issued long-term infrastructure development project bonds in order to finance the country's infrastructure development project. Those 10-year bonds were of such types where there used to be coupon payments annually along with 10 years of maturity period. These had low risks, hence attract investors, since their issuers' credit ratings had remained good with support of state government guarantees. This has constantly been repaying the principal for all the years leading up to this current year as a source of steady investment to the investors regardless of the economic recession or fluctuations of the economy, thus bond investments are reliable. From the proceeds of its issue, it invested in building roads and utilities; thereby, showing how the issuing corporation also assists in the development process while satisfying investor requirements.

Questions

1. Why are bonds considered low-investment risk? Explain the case under study how they have been able to maintain this position:

2. How do bonds contribute to economic development according to the case study?

Case Study: Mutual Funds

This diversified mutual fund in India has emerged as a favorite among investors for its well-balanced investment strategy, which focuses on equity and debt instruments. This mutual fund has provided pretty consistent returns over the last five years, with many market conditions being beaten. Professional management by the fund helped reduce all risks through diversified investment opportunities in sectors like technology, healthcare, and infrastructure. An investor, for example, who had started with an SIP of a very low sum every month ended up amassing substantial wealth; this is what discipline investing can do. Translucency and regular updates provided another reason for the boost of confidence among investors to look forward to the accomplishment of their financial goals under the management of professionals.

Questions:

1. How does mutual fund diversification reduce risk, and how do professionals help in doing so?
2. Advantages of opening SIP with which have been addressed in the following case in point

These case studies bring into evidence the importance of bonds and mutual funds in a portfolio, which provides both stability and growth potential. Examples like these will illustrate for the undergraduate student and the novice investor how these financial instruments help create long-term wealth while being aligned to risk preferences.

3.3 INDIA REGULATION AND TRANSPARENCY.

In India, mutual funds are regulated by the Securities and Exchange Board of India. This regulating organization ensures that the financial industry operates transparently and honestly. This is because SEBI's detailed criteria require fund firms to make information about their portfolio, fees, and performance available. Thus, transparency in this domain is required to empower an investor with knowledge that may be used to make well-informed decisions and to trust the mutual fund ecosystem.

SEBI mandates mutual funds to issue periodic statements on its holdings, NAVs, and expense ratios. All of this information allows investors to analyze performance against other choices available in the market. An investor may view the history of a fund's returns and which sectors the fund invested in, as well as costs associated with such a fund, before entrusting money to that fund. It reduces information asymmetry and holds the fund manager accountable.

In addition, SEBI has harsh measures of compliance to ensure investor interests. These measures involve setting certain limits for investment in specified sectors or securities, ensuring sufficient diversification, and avoiding over-risky situations. For instance, funds should meet an agreed investment target in line with the interest of their investors.

Public awareness campaigns, like "Mutual Funds Sahi Hai," have furthered the cause of increasing transparency by educating the investor on the benefits of mutual funds and the importance of due diligence. These initiatives result in a steady growth trend with confidence among retail investors entering the mutual fund industry.

Overall, SEBI's regulatory framework has played a pivotal role in enhancing the credibility of mutual funds in India. By prioritizing transparency and investor protection, SEBI has created an environment where individuals can safely and effectively participate in wealth creation through mutual funds.

Relevance in India

This shift has happened in India's financial sector with increasing financial literacy, rising adoption of digital channels, and an increasingly active regulatory environment. It has inspired more Indians to invest in financial products such as bonds and mutual funds for their financial purposes. Today, with online platforms and mobile apps, investment has become accessible even for the people of small towns and rural areas.

Government bonds and debt funds now come in as the next most sought-after investment product by the risk-averse investor. These instruments do offer stability and predictable returns on investments, making them ideal to be preserved while earning a steady income. Whereas equity funds and hybrid funds appeal to the moderate risk-taker investor who seeks higher growth by getting exposure to equity markets and diversified portfolios. Public awareness campaigns, like "Mutual Funds Sahi Hai," have played a very vital role in popularizing investments in mutual funds. This campaign stresses the importance of getting started early, investing systematically, and leveraging professional management to build long-term wealth. The introduction of SIPs has made mutual fund investments very accessible, allowing people to invest small, regular amounts, thereby fostering a culture of disciplined savings. One of the most important steps towards financial independence and security for students and new investors is the subtlety of bonds and mutual funds. These instruments lay the base for a well-balanced portfolio, aligning with diversified financial goals and risk preferences. The knowledge of these markets, if learned and practiced actively, helps people exploit the potential of financial instruments to grow wealth systematically.

To summarize, bonds and mutual funds are integral parts of India's financial system, providing multiple choices to suit different objectives of investment. As India continues its journey toward becoming an economic superpower in the world, the importance of these instruments will only rise, making them essential instruments for wealth creation and economic participation.

3.4 THE FUNDAMENTALS OF CRYPTOCURRENCIES

Cryptocurrencies are a new genre of digital currencies that transformed the financial world in the past few years. Unlike paper currencies, which are issued and maintained by central banks, cryptos are digital or virtual currencies secured by advanced methods of cryptography. This method of security resists counterfeiting and fraud so that users have a considerable amount of trust in transactions with it.

The decentralized nature of networks is one characteristic trait of cryptocurrencies. They run on the Blockchain technology distributed ledger system that records transactions on many computers. Blockchain eradicates the need to have intermediaries such as banks or payment processors in a transaction process. Transactions have thus proven to be faster, more efficient, and low cost. All the transactions on a blockchain network ensure transparency and immutability, thus giving it security and accountability to the system.

The first and most well-known among these was Bitcoin, which was started in 2009 by an individual or group known under the pseudonym Satoshi Nakamoto. Bitcoin was one of the first peer-to-peer digital currencies that was created to replace traditional financial systems; it became successful and soon thousands more cryptocurrencies, collectively known as altcoins, were developed in total. Some of the popular altcoins include Ethereum, Ripple (XRP), and Litecoin, among others.

For example, Ethereum is more than just a digital currency because it supports smart contracts or self-executing agreements directly with terms written into the code. This has revolutionized many aspects of life, including in decentralized finance, where completely novel financial products and services could now materialize without the requirement of employing traditional intermediaries, like Ripple (XRP), that centers on its objective of quick and inexpensive cross-border transactions, mainly directed toward companies that focus on international trade.

3.4.1 Cryptocurrencies Benefits

Some of the advantages that cryptocurrencies offer have made them popular and more adopted. The following are key advantages of cryptocurrencies in greater detail:

1. **Decentralization:** Cryptocurrencies are operated on decentralized networks, and therefore, there is no central authority controlling them such as a bank or government. Decentralization decreases the possibility of censorship or manipulation and thus provides users with complete control over their financial assets. For instance, decentralized cryptocurrencies guarantee that users can send and receive funds even in regions with unstable financial systems or restrictive government policies.
2. **Low Transaction Costs:** Traditional finance system incurs much in fees and more especially with the transfer of international money across intermediaries like banks and payment processors. The cryptocurrency enables direct person to person transfer which, thereby significantly saves costs. An example of this is where international transfers are usually coupled with only a few cents fees and, thereby save the process in the transfer process of remittances.
3. **Speed of transactions:** Cryptocurrency transactions are processed within a few minutes regardless of the geographical position of the sender and the receiver. This is different in the case of traditional bank systems where international transfers take a number of days. For example, cross-border payments done using Bitcoin or Ripple would be processed in a far smaller fraction of time consumed by conventional means.
4. **Financial Inclusion:** Cryptocurrency helps financially accommodate over billions of unbanked and underbanked population globally. With just access to the internet and a digital wallet, a person becomes included in the world of the financial ecosystem. This is most transformative in rural or underdeveloped regions where this banking structure is not in existence or simply absent in place.

5. **Transparency and Security**: Transactions carried on a cryptocurrency, based on blockchain technology, are registered on the public ledger, so everything remains transparent. That minimizes fraud risk and enhances reliability. What is more, sophisticated encryption methods secure transactions in a way that hackers cannot even hack into a user's account to withdraw his/her money or any information of a user.
6. **Access:** It is relatively easy to get cryptocurrencies. For cryptocurrencies, one requires just an internet connection and a digital wallet, but the traditional banking system requires for a bank account and tonnes of paper. It makes any person, in any financial situation, capable of investing, saving, or even transferring money due to this simple access, which democratizes financial instruments.
7. **Programmable Abilities:** In the case of currencies like Ethereum, smart contracts are automated agreements that run when a certain condition is met. Such a contract would automatically remove the middlemen, hence allowing higher prospects of supply chain management, tokenized assets, and decentralized financing. For example, the automation of rental agreements through smart contracts will remove administrative burdens but make it more efficient.
8. **Portfolio Diversification:** The best thing about cryptocurrencies is the opportunity to diversify portfolios. It is a relatively new asset class, so the performance is not correlated directly with stocks or bonds. That means adding cryptocurrencies helps in managing risks and possibly getting better returns in volatile markets.
9. **Privacy and Anonymity:** The blockchain technology is transparent, but in the context of cryptocurrencies, transactions do not directly link addresses with identities of the users; therefore, it is somewhat private. This feature will appeal to those who want to have financial privacy. Note that this anonymity is pseudonymous. Sophisticated analysis might trace transactions back to the users if there is a need for such tracing.
10. **Growth and Innovation Opportunity:** The cryptocurrencies have actually fueled the growth of the technology, especially when focusing on blockchain, cybersecurity, or even applications. In addition, the growth perspective related to blockchain technology can easily be portrayed by NFTs or DeFi. The appeal to developers or even businesses or investors considering embracing new opportunities might therefore very much depend on this fact.

3.4.2 Dangers of the Cryptocurrencies

While cryptocurrencies present exciting opportunities, there are several risks they carry that potential users and investors should be aware of. Those risks are discussed in depth below.

1. **Price Volatility:** Cryptocurrencies are known for their wild price fluctuations. Their value can change drastically within hours or days due to market speculation, regulatory announcements, and technological advancements. For instance, the price of Bitcoin skyrocketed to record highs before crashing within weeks. Such volatility makes cryptocurrencies a high-risk asset, unsuitable for conservative investors or those seeking steady returns.
2. **Regulatory Uncertainty:** In many countries, the legality of cryptocurrencies is unclear- even in India. It is legal in some nations; others strictly regulate or entirely prohibit it.For India, policymakers are yet to decide the framework regarding the regulation of cryptocurrencies and, hence, create an uncertainty for business and investment. Such a lack of clarity might be a dampener to investments and restrict the growth of innovation concerning cryptocurrencies.
3. **Security Risks:** Blockchain itself is highly secure. The only thing is that trading of cryptocurrency is usually held through a few platforms and exchanges which often happen to be under attacks. Millions of dollars' worth of breach at a cryptocurrency exchange because of hacking and several other such losses occurred because of hacking, resulting in permanent loss due to private keys lost due to users losing access.
4. **Absence of Consumer Protection**:Unlike traditional financial systems, the decentralized nature of cryptocurrencies lacks centralized control. The lack of regulation leaves the user with limited means to seek redress in cases of fraud, hacking, or disputes. For example, if a cryptocurrency exchange is declared

bankrupt or engages in dubious activities, it will be nearly impossible for the users to recover their money. This forms an added risk in the shape of a lack of consumer protection.

5. **Scalability Issues.** Most of the cryptocurrencies suffer from a large number of transactions inefficiently. Networks like Bitcoin and Ethereum are normally congested at peak times. This results in slow speeds of transaction, more charges, and thus can not compete with mainstream payment systems on a big scale especially for everyday transactions.
6. **Environmental Issues:** The energy-intensive process of mining cryptocurrency, particularly proof-of-work (PoW) cryptocurrencies such as Bitcoin, has raised significant environmental issues. The computational strength needed to mine the currency translates directly into energy use. In cases where electricity is mainly generated using fossil fuels, the cryptocurrency mining process contributes to greenhouse gas emissions, which seems to raise the question about its sustainability.
7. **Market Manipulation**: Crypto markets, in its state of being somewhat decontrolled, can easily get hijacked by major players popularly known as "whales." They have a profound say over prices; that is why it allows massive pump-and-dump action - boosting prices and then slashing, leaving small-time traders suffering huge losses.
8. **Lack of Knowledge and Education:** Cryptocurrency is an elaborate financial tool that very few people actually know and understand how they work or their underlying technologies. Few know the risks they bring. These are main factors in leading to unwise investments and susceptibility to frauds. Education campaigns would greatly determine people making better investment decisions.
9. **Opportunity for Illicit Activities:** The anonymity features of the cryptocurrency make it attractive to people engaging in illicit activities like money laundering, tax evasion, and purchasing illegal goods. While most the cryptocurrency transactions are legitimate, negative associations can harm the public perception and lead to tougher regulatory measures that will inhibit innovation.
10. **Reversible Transactions.** Cryptocurrency transactions are irreversible. A person never gets the money transferred to the wrong address or fraudulent entity. This aspect creates complexity and adds caution for the users, in particular those who are unacquainted with this technology. Accuracy in making transactions and watchfulness towards scams is the key.

Cryptocurrencies are a very unique blend of opportunities and challenges in the modern financial landscape. The innovative features - decentralization, transparency, and accessibility - hold a high potential to revolutionize the whole way of functioning of financial systems. Enabling financial inclusion, promoting technological advancement, and changing traditional notions about money and investment are but a few examples of this reshaping.

Though volatility may be a risk factor involving uncontrolled price swings, security vulnerabilities, and regulatory hazards, there are downsides to cryptocurrencies. Investors must understand that the fact a cryptocurrency offers huge rewards can never be without considerable dangers. An equally well-rewarded strategy is warranted to avoid all potential disadvantages.

The best way to really understand a cryptocurrency system is by first focusing on proper research regarding the subtleties that this new asset class entails. Good security will start by protecting private keys and utilizing trusted platforms to safeguard the investment. Users who know more about regulation changes and market trends will be much better decision-makers.

Short speaking, the cryptocurrencies stand for the possibility of change in financial life and demand participation responsibly. Through embracing the innovation, which also provides solutions to the challenges created, the users and investors can play a role in sustainable growth and integration into the world economy.

Applicability to India

India's financial markets are undergoing rapid changes due to the robust growth in the economy, technology, and more active investors. This group includes Bombay Stock Exchange and National Stock Exchange among the largest stock exchanges by market capitalization in the world. This reflects an increasingly important role that India's equity markets play in facilitating economic growth and providing scope for creating wealth. As more Indian companies go public, the equity market continues to attract domestic as well as international investors and thus plays a key role in world finance.

India has witnessed tremendous growth in the mutual fund industry over the last ten years. Assets under management (AUM) are at unprecedented levels, mainly due to the recognition of advantages when people invest in diversified portfolios of investment opportunities being managed by professionals in finance. The democratization of the market by Systematic Investment Plans has made mutual funds easily accessible to small, routine investments by ordinary Indian citizens in building long-term wealth. This approach has significantly enhanced the financial literacy of the masses and made saving and investment a more popular culture for the newer generations.

There is increased interest in India too in cryptos, as a growing number of enthusiasts and investors explore this nascent asset class. With regulatory ambiguities, India continues to be among the largest adoption markets of cryptocurrencies. There is significant popularity in the trading of cryptocurrencies, thereby enabling greater access to this innovative financial technology. Regulators are developing frameworks to govern cryptocurrency usage, including the Reserve Bank of India and other government agencies. These developments aim to balance the need to protect investors with the importance of fostering innovation in blockchain technology beyond cryptocurrency usage-considering applications in supply chain management and digital identity verification, for example.

The study of financial markets and instruments is mandatory for anyone seeking to steer the country's fast-changing financial landscape. For an investor, it forms a tool for decision making in augmenting his or her wealth with safety. To professional aspirants, this helps one explore the sector, for example, investment banking, portfolio management, and financial technology. Knowledge about developments in the financial markets is critical in India's rapidly changing economy for effective harnessing of opportunities and reduction of risk.

Financial markets and instruments are the spine of the Indian economy since they provide avenues for the flow of capital, induce investment, and create wealth. In these three steps of finance- one needs to understand all such principles not only for acquiring academic excellence but also making better financial decisions, that will contribute towards the overall economic growth of the nation. With the modernization of the financial ecosystem of India, these concepts shall grow in relevance and are indispensable for the future.

How to Get Started

There is much to learn for students looking to break into the financial markets and instruments. Learning the basics and being hands-on in the approach will work best for them. Here are some actionable steps and resources that can get students started:

1. Learning Platforms for Stock Trading

- Low-cost or free stock market simulators and virtual platforms for trading, starting with these helps a learner trade risk-free, but they learn by actually performing on the markets.
- Real-time data, tutorial, and market analysis software is also a great deal for understanding stock trading basic concepts. Look for platforms with resources, information, and user-friendly interfaces that are specifically designed for novices.

2. Resources to learn about mutual funds

- Start with the resources provided by regulatory agencies on their websites, such as SEBI. Many of them have FAQs and investment rules for first-time investors.

- Find financial education portals that discuss the basics of mutual funds, including how SIPs function. Many fund houses provide educational content to help one understand various types of funds and their risk-return profiles.
- Use the mutual fund comparison sites in tracking the past performance of these funds, fees paid, and the composition of their portfolios.

3. Precautions to Enter the Cryptocurrency Market

- Research on well-reviewed cryptocurrency exchange sites on points of security, transparency and compliance to law. Use caution when looking out not to engage on very porous exchanges with questionable policies.
- Know that one is exposing his investments in cryptocurrency to specific inherent risks such as volatile price ranges and regulatory vagueness. Make informed choices while using reputable resource like Blockchain explainer guide, online courses for investors among many others.
- Never invest more than you can afford to lose. Cryptocurrency markets are highly speculative, and newbie investors should enter these markets cautiously with small amounts.

General Tips on All Markets

- Know What's Going On: Read news, market updates, and trends about the financial instruments you care most about. Some good sources for financial news and in-depth market analysis blogs.
- Set Clear Goals: Setting your financial goals and risk tolerance, as well as your investment timeline, gives you a clear direction before you start. This further enables you to select ideal instruments, whether stocks, bonds, mutual funds, or cryptocurrencies.
- Seek Advice: Never be hesitant to seek advice from finance experts and mentors. Most educational institutes and financial service providers even provide workshops, webinars, and one-on-one advisory sessions for beginners.

It takes a student small starts, staying informed, and being disciplined to have that skill and confidence required for effective maneuvering of financial markets. This lays down the foundation for long-term financial literacy and success.

CHAPTER 4

DIGITAL BANKING AND PAYMENT SOLUTIONS

4.1 INTRODUCTION

These digital banking and payment solutions have transformed the interface between people and financial services, as well as with businesses, in many fundamental ways. In a world that emphasizes speed, convenience, and security, these innovations fill a gap between what older banking systems could do and consumer expectations in this new millennium. From only accessing online accounts to using mobile phones to make instant transactions, digital banking, and payment solutions have made access to financial services the most inclusive in history.

Digital banking is a very wide range of services, allowing users to do their banking activities without having to visit the physical branches. These services comprise online transfers, bill payments, loan applications, and investment tracking. Payment solutions include mobile wallets and payment gateways that complement these services by providing cashless transactions for personal purchases or business operations. All these combines into a seamless ecosystem that really enhances the user experience.

Technological advances and the resultant policy pushes in digital banking and payment solutions have catapulted off well in India. These have truly taken a massive boost in Digital India, UPI, and the cashless economy, with this digital approach becoming easier for adoption. In those places that traditionally have seen minimal usage of physical infrastructure by way of traditional banks, this was able to become easy in digital, too, while incorporating easy options towards achieving financial inclusion.

Smartphones and widely spread connectivity are necessities; they have opened the door to accessibility to financial tools for all walks of people. For example, an investor in a remote rural setting can have his money remitted directly into the wallet or account of such person, thereby eliminating any intermediary through which a delay might occur. Mobile payment solutions are similarly transforming small enterprises to grow larger and become more productive also.

Knowledge in today's environment has become a necessity for the student and the young professional using digital banking and payment systems. This is the foundation of improving financial independence, managing personal money, and eventually accumulating wealth. In today's technologically changing global economy, knowledge also gives one a competitive edge in professions involving finance, technology, and entrepreneurship.

This chapter covers the essential elements of digital banking and payment systems. These would be: focuses on online banking platforms, mobile payments and wallets, and payment gateways. In fact, through an analysis of features, benefits, and actual applications, readers would become quite familiar with how such technologies are changing the landscape in finance. Practical examples and case studies will help the student to understand the relevance in the rapidly changing financial ecosystem in India and get the students ready to navigate and use these innovations well.

4.2 ONLINE BANKING PLATFORMS

Online banking platforms have changed the financial management for the individual and business at a very basic level. Such platforms allow access to most banking services throughout the day, and they do not depend on the availability of physical branches. The customer can conduct transactions, check accounts, and pay bills from home or the workplace. Key features include transfer of funds, bill payments, tracking investments, and real-time monitoring of transactions. In place are serious advanced technology security measures, including two-factor authentication, encrypted protocols, and fraud-detection systems, which further ensures that user data never leaks out.

In the Indian context, the main driving force behind the implementation of online banking has been the availability of low-priced handsets and improvement of net connectivity.

With this advancement in technology, more and more people and businesses have been able to access the financial services. Online banking has reached out to many diverse groups of people that address specific needs while also improving financial inclusion and participation in the economy across the country.

Urban Professionals

For the urban professionals, online banking is offering resources for the management of their finances. Users can now make use of online banking tools ranging from tracking investments, automated bill payments, and personal financial advice through simple interfaces. In this respect, dependence on physical visits to banks has reduced the time taken and increased the convenience levels for the tech-savvy population managing complex financial portfolios.

Rural Entrepreneurs

Online banking platforms have been a game changer for small business owners in rural areas. They include online banking services like microlending and digital wallets in their integration, through which cash flow management, scaling operation, and investing in the growth of businesses are easy. For example, the people in rural areas can, from their smartphones, straight away apply for loans cutting through the bureaucratic procedures into the funds they may have needed.

Promote financial inclusion

Digital wallets and micro-financing facilities are major drivers for India towards financial inclusion. These facilities specifically cater to the rural and semi-urban populations, and thus the otherwise excluded individuals have been empowered with it. Thus now, the farmer will obtain his subsidy or payment upon his crop directly into the bank account instead of becoming a middleman dependent and only to get paid when a middleman finds it convenient for himself to pay him. Example Take a farmer residing in a small village, has access through an online banking system. It has got a digital wallet. Using UPI, the farmer can receive money for their produce and the same online banking platform for payment of seeds and fertilizers. Furthermore, using micro-loans available on the net, the farmer may invest in better equipment that would help him to become more productive and increase income.

The online banking revolution in India has now bridged the gap between being in the city and on a rural plain, making access to financial empowerment much more accessible. Thus, with innovative, bespoke features that meet all such needs, these interfaces will drive financial inclusion toward greater economic growth and contribute toward the development of this country.

For students, online banking provides important benefits that make the management of personal finance easy and even allow access to educational loans or scholarships without the hassle of traditional paperwork. Most of the platforms also have budgeting tools and expense trackers that will help young users develop financial literacy.

Example: A college student who lives in a semi-urban locality keeps track of his monthly budget on an online banking site. The part-time income he earns enables him to transfer the amount to pay for the tuition fees, track all his expenses in real time, and even set saving goals. Furthermore, the entire process of obtaining an education loan was completely online. He did not need to visit any branch at all. This facilitated comfort gave him ample time for academics while taking care of the money.

Online banking platforms have streamlined financial transactions while at the same time improving economic participation from all walks of society. With technology on the horizon, these platforms will continue to play a very significant role in financial empowerment and inclusion.

Example Case Study: A young business owner operated the online banking platform to monitor the finances of an e-commerce company. This platform, in addition to accounting software, enabled automatic production of invoices and reconciliation of payments. The cash flow was better managed, and this reduced the human error to a greater extent. This saved an enormous amount of time for that entrepreneur.

The entrepreneur used analytics tools on the platform to monitor expenses and optimize resources, which explains how the versatility of online banking platforms helps in the support of small businesses.

Online banking platforms are quickly becoming the foundation of the new digital-first economy. They are more efficient, convenient, and secure than ever. The relevance of such platforms will increase with evolution and gaining more central roles in boosting financial literacy, financial inclusion, and economic growth.

4.3 WALLETS AND MOBILE PAYMENTS

Digital wallets and mobile payments became a new pillar in the online economy. They changed financial transactions totally. The mentioned solutions ensure that the execution of any transaction will become simple and comfortable both for personal and business purposes using cashless transactions by the cell phones.

Money transfer among peers, payment to merchants, and settlements of utility bills become things of the past because no cash or cards are needed. The usage of QR codes, contactless payments, and one-click transactions has increased further usability, which can benefit a wide range of users.

Mobile payments have become a very widely adopted phenomenon in India due to synergy in technological advancements and facilitating government policies. Thus, the Unified Payments Interface has transformed digital payments by enabling instant, secure, and bank-to-bank fund transfers without asking for the full details of account information. Interoperability ensures that the transactions are seamless, hence constituting the cornerstone of India's push toward a cashless economy.

4.3.1 Key Drivers of Adoption

1. Government Initiatives

Of course, the Indian government has played a significant role in promoting mobile payments as well as digital wallets through its initiatives like Digital India and regulations in place on cashless transactions and that accompanying infrastructure which is to form the bedrock for a proper digital payment climate. Instantaneous fund transfers between banks, which was possible with the Unified Payments Interface initiated by the government, have nullified the usage of the traditional payment mode. Further, initiatives like PMJDY have brought financial inclusion that made millions of unbanked people turn to digital payment alternatives. This further brings about a facilitative atmosphere for mobile wallets where every citizen can make digital payment at any tier of society.

2. Smartphone Penetration

Smart phones have been very cheap and data packages equally low in India, making smartphone penetration the game changer for mobile payments in India. This technology reaches all nooks and corners of the country as internet connectivity has ensured mobile payment technologies are at everyone's fingertips, with those living in rural or semi-urban areas using smartphones equipped with intuitive interfaces, making it possible to execute digital transactions without banking infrastructure. This democratization of technology not only expands the use of mobile wallets but accelerates their adoption in underserved regions with limited access to more traditional banking services.

3. **Ease of use**

Novel features and mobile payment technology have made the same accessible to a considerable range of demographics, with some using it even though they hardly have any technical literacy. One-click payments, scanning of QR codes, contactless transactions have made things less complicated and therefore, less of an entry barrier. Voice-guided payment systems in regional languages add another layer of usability for those who are not comfortable speaking in English. These features ensure that even those people who are not familiar with advanced technology can easily access mobile wallets, thus furthering financial inclusion and wider adoption.

Hence, as is obvious, these key drivers have, in concert with each other, worked collectively to accelerate the growth in mobile payments and digital wallets. They reflect the harmonious integration of technology and policy that facilitates accessible usage in transforming the mode and manner of financial transactions for the Indian people.

Example: A street vendor selling in a small town embraced the mobile wallet to acquire payments from those who need to make electronic transactions with the customers. Displaying a QR code will facilitate quick and safe payments and will increase the daily sale and avoid large cash, hence reducing chances of getting stolen and will simplify its accounting.

4.3.2 Key Features and Benefits

1. Peer-to-Peer Transfers:

It makes sending money directly to friends or family easy without depending on cash, checks, or going to the bank. In just a few clicks of a smartphone, users can split a bill, pay off a loan, or send assistance to loved ones in minutes. Shared rental apartment students can easily split the bill with the help of the peer-to-peer transfer feature. These are transactions that are immediate, very convenient, especially on small day-to-day kinds of transactions and reduce the inconvenience of dealing with traditional money handling.

2. Merchants

Mobile wallets are increasingly becoming popular among informal traders, street vendors among others. This way they can be able to have smooth receipt of digital transactions, therefore reducing their usage of cash and increasing business efficiency. This would enable merchants to cater to more customers who would like to avoid cash transactions. For instance, the street food vendor can now satisfy the tech-savvy urban customer by enabling the latter to pay digitally. This reduces risks in cash handling and provides a better experience for customers.

3. Utility Bill Payments

Mobile wallets allow one to pay utility bills instantly and securely, such as electricity, water, and even mobile recharges. Therefore, there is no more visiting payment centers or fearing late fees; it saves both time and effort, and users can even remind themselves or automate payments not to miss any due dates. For example, a working professional can pay several household bills during his or her lunch break, which would save him or her much time in his or her daily schedule and would ensure uninterrupted services.

4. Contactless Payments:

Use of NFC (Near Field Communication) technology has allowed transaction systems to become easier contactlessly. This way, individuals can make payments without direct contact between their devices; they simply tap on any compatible payment terminal by way of their smartphones for swift and hygienic ways of doing things, making it ideal for environments with high volumes, like grocers, where this counts the most. The advancement of contactless also further enhances security since card fraud or theft of a pin number becomes less vulnerable as well.

These features, in combination, make mobile wallets an absolute necessity in the digital economy. Convenience, security, and versatility combine to allow for a broad range of use cases that change how people and businesses deal with their transactions.

4.4 IMPACT ON URBAN AND RURAL INDIA

1. Urban Areas:

Mobile wallets have perfectly fit into the lifestyle of the urban tech-savvy. They are faster and more convenient than anything else. Urban consumers are using mobile wallets for ride-sharing services, dining out, online shopping, and utility bill payments. Completing a transaction just with a smartphone has made mobile wallets the most popular mode of payment for millennials and working professionals. For example, today ride-sharing services integrate with wallet payments for an ease of cashless, stress-free commuting through bustling cities.

2. Rural Areas

Mobile wallets have become the primary mode of connectivity between traditional banking and the modern financial services sector for semi-urban and rural areas. Areas like this are generally less developed regarding infrastructure. It is, therefore difficult to access the financial system. Using mobile wallets allows one to make payments and receive government subsidies, doing basic banking with little need to visit a physical branch. For example, farmers in rural villages can now receive payments directly into their mobile wallets. This ensures faster and safer transactions while reducing dependency on cash.

1. Younger users:

Mobile wallets are the latest trend among Gen Z and millennials, who love using speedy and easy mobile wallets for the first time as digital financial instruments. Such customers are always attracted to reward points and cashback offers and instant payouts. Other examples of how young people increasingly rely on digital-first solutions for their fast-paced lifestyles include splitting restaurant bills and making purchases online. Wallet interfaces that are gamified-for example, by giving badges for prudent spending or saving-become even more popular with this age group.

2. Adoption in Rural Areas

Mobile wallets have, no doubt, transformed financial inclusion in rural and semi-urban areas by providing a convenient substitute for cash.

Many people in semi-urban and rural areas do not have bank accounts but possess smart phones; mobile wallets help them in accessing their financial necessities. Regional language support and voice-guided instructions are some of the features that have contributed to making these platforms adoptable by people with relatively low digital literacy. This, therefore, means governments use mobile wallets in the distribution and management of government subsidies to ensure greater financial inclusion.

3. Government Support

It is along these lines of efforts of the Indian government through the initiatives like Digital India and its launching of the Unified Payments Interface (UPI) that mobile wallets have seen some adoption. The digital payment ecosystem has been built in a robust, secure, and interoperable transaction. The digital payment landscape has thus been revolutionized with instant, cost-effective, and seamless fund transfers enabled through UPI. Government campaigns for cashless transactions speed up the transition while making sure that mobile wallets reach even the most distant corners of the country.

The impact of mobile wallets is transformative in India, from cities to rural areas and has been able to provide varied user needs. Mobile wallets enable financial inclusion, create an economic participatory effect, and increase digital literacy and are reshaping the entire financial ecosystem of India. Their role to the digital economy of India would become very significant with the continuous technology advancement and government support.

As an example, a supermarket in a small rural town decided to accept mobile payments from its customers, most of whom were not connected to conventional banking systems.

Adding a QR code connected to an e-wallet enabled the owner of the store to alter the nature of transactions. Cash became useless as customers were able to pay instantly by scanning the QR code on their cellphones. This increased the efficiency of transactions and attracted more clients who preferred electronic payment methods.

The people in the local community felt the change. Cash croppers began using cellphones. This made them rely less on physical currency and reduced the risks of carrying such cash, introducing them instead to the greater benefits digital financial tools offer. The business owner experienced smooth operations in addition to faster settlement payments, which improved overall performance.

Digital wallets and mobile payments revolutionize the process of making transactions in disadvantaged communities with no financial infrastructure. In this regard, these technologies help to achieve the aim of a cashless economy, boost economic growth, and promote inclusiveness in financial services. With more customers and businesses adopting these solutions, India is gradually inching toward becoming a digitally empowered society in which convenience and innovation propel everyday transactions.

Case Study: A small shop in a rural town realized the increasing demands for cashless transactions. The shop owner, serving many of the local farmers and daily wage workers, realized that these customers cannot always access physical cash as there is no banking infrastructure in the area. This made it easy for the customers to pay through their smartphones by including a mobile wallet payment system with QR codes.

This transition brought multiple benefits to business. First, it massively enhanced customer satisfaction because their transaction could now be quick and secure without having any money on them. Further, it increased the business shop's customer base that attracts tech-savvy youngsters and other customers for its digital payments. At the same time, the cash flow of the owner came without any hassles about taking cash to banks or making change on-site.

Mobile wallet payments increased the sales of the shop. They made more purchases because electronic payments eliminated cash constraints. It became a local example of how technology can drive business growth and improve service delivery in rural areas.

This case study, therefore, points towards the possibility of transformation in the mobile payment solution while building financial inclusion and boosting the economic activity mainly in economically disadvantaged areas of limited financial services.

4.5 PAYMENT GATEWAYS

Payment gateways are critical for the success of any online transaction. They serve as intermediaries that can guarantee secure payment processing between the buyer and the merchant. They ensure that funds are transferred smoothly while keeping card information and personal data confidential using robust encryption techniques. Thus, payment gateways can ensure that both the buyer and seller have trust in digital commerce through safe transactions.

4.5.1 Main Functionalities of Payment Gateways

1. Multi-Currency Support:

Payment gateways are essential for any business in a global marketplace. They will support multi-currency facilities for merchants to accept all forms of payments in terms of different currencies. Customers around the world can use their currency comfortably to enjoy easy and smooth transactions. For example, an Indian craftsman selling his products online can take payments from the customers in the United States or Europe in their local currency, which would make it easier and reach more people in the business.

2.Fraud Detection And Prevention:

What matters most in online transaction is security, and payment gateways make use of advanced fraud detection systems that protect both merchants and customers. Tools such as machine learning algorithms analyze transaction patterns to identify anomalies, and real-time monitoring flags suspicious activities instantly. For instance, when an unusual location for a credit card transaction is made or exceeds the normal limit of spending, the payment gateway may stop the transaction; thus, it may stop possible fraud. These systems do not only reduce loss but also build trust by the user because they protect the information of the clients.

3.Integration with E-commerce Websites:

Payment gateways can integrate with other e-commerce websites seamlessly. Therefore, businesses can offer several payment options to the customers, such as credit/debit cards, digital wallets, UPI, and net banking. This results in smooth checkout processes for customers and reduces cart abandonment rates. For example, an e-retailer would be able to provide various modes of payment, so as to cater to the tastes of a customer through an integrated payment gateway. Besides, automated reconciliation saves back-end processes to a large extent, thus leaving enough time for merchants to be involved in the growth of the business.

Payment gateway systems are more than just simple transactions. It supports various currencies, makes security by fraudulent activities and has compatibility with e-commerce websites, etc. For all these features, business is equipped with the digital economy and students and up-and-coming entrepreneurs must know about these features so that they can effectively make use of payment gateways for their business ventures.

Impact in India

Indian pay and accepted payment gateways have streamlined financial transactions between businesses, customers, and banks that make them play a cardinal role in the fast pacing digital transformation of India. The systems have helped nurture the growth of online commerce and digital services by alleviating gaps in traditional finance infrastructure and empowering small enterprises in equal measure.

1. Empowering Small Businesses and Local Artisans

Payment gateways completely changed the existing dynamics through which smaller businesses and regional craftspeople function, creating the possibility of reaching a much larger audience beyond geographical limitations. While these small businesses were earlier operating on cash basis or through local markets, payment gateway may now be utilized to digitize its collections through bank transfers, digital wallets, and UPI. With no actual currency required, logistical hurdles are removed and the operational efficiency is increased.

Doing away with the use of actual currency means to remove logistical barriers and promote operational efficiency.For instance, an e-commerce platform has enabled a far-flung hamlet artisan to sell handcrafted products to consumers all over India. Traditional payment mechanisms would have resulted in delays, but the inclusion of a payment gateway by the e-commerce platform ensures that the artisan is paid safely and immediately. This ease of transaction boosts client happiness and confidence, making clients come back again and again. Online selling encourages entrepreneurism because artists will spend more time on creating and less time with technology executing a transaction. Such democratization of financial tools broadens business participation and contributes to bridging the gap between the urban and rural.

2. Supporting the Freelancing Ecosystem

With this development comes the increase in dependency on payment gateways in financial transactions. It offers an easy, effective means of handling services of transactions to the advantage of all freelancers, even those students working part-time or remotely. This way, payment gateways allow seamless receipt of payments from clients globally, thereby allowing freelancers to work freely without being hindered by physical border lines.

Thus, if a graphic designer in India completes a project for a client overseas, he can be assured of getting instant, secure payment through a payment gateway, usually in the currency of the client. The systems eliminate most of the complexities that occur with international transactions, like high transfer fees or processing times. Thirdly, transparency in a payment gateway transaction tracking and detailed payment histories-helps freelancers in financial planning and record-keeping.

The removal of barriers to entry in the global marketplace encourages more people to join the digital economy. Accessibility promotes financial independence, and students and professionals become empowered to monetize their skills, which contribute to the growth of the freelancing ecosystem in India and all over the world.

3. Accelerating E-Commerce Growth

Indian e-commerce has grown at a rapid rate with payment gateways in the center of the revolution. These systems form the back bone of online businesses by ensuring safe and efficient payments to a diverse customer base. From new startups to large enterprises, the process of transaction through a payment gateway makes the transactions smoother, which is one way that improves the customer experience overall.

Multi-currency support, fraud detection, and integration with the shopping platform are features with the maximum impact to let businesses become effective in a digital marketplace. For instance, an online clothing start-up will use a payment gateway for UPI, credit/debit cards, and digital wallets provided for the customers. Meaning seamless checkout, lesser cart abandonment, and high retention.

Another reason payment gateways enable cross-border trade is in terms of acceptance of payments in other currencies, which widens the merchant's market reach into international markets. They have emerged as a vital technology tool for businesses to prosper in India's very competitive e-commerce industry since these systems satisfy some of the most critical needs: namely, transaction security and ease of use. Their role in building trust and convenience has significantly added up to the exponential growth of online shopping in the country.

4. Deepen Financial Inclusion

In semi-urban and rural locations, where traditional banking infrastructure is not fully accessible, payment gateways serve as an alternative tool that enables financial inclusion. It connects small vendors, shopkeepers, and service providers who can now take digital payments, thus placing them on the formal financial system. This shift to a cashless transaction is also more efficient and safer due to less risk of handling and storing big amounts of cash.

Take an example of a small, nondescript roadside tea shop in a rural village - it can now take its customers who wish to do digital payments with the use of a payment gateway with a UPI support. Thus, it saves operational overheads in the form of cash handling and gives safety and ease of payment options to customers. Payment gateway also allows local businesses to compete with urban markets while bridging the gap for rural economic participation with its urban counterpart.

These are one of the cornerstones of India's digital economy, as they enable secure and efficient transactions that help benefit businesses as much as individuals. Right from enabling small artisans to tap into national markets, these systems are driving economic growth and financial inclusion-from supporting freelancers in the gig economy. And it continues to play a core part in the financial landscape of the entire country as that march towards a digitally empowered nation persists.

The acceleration of this trend has become so great that even the most remote areas of the country have access to digital payments, thanks to the Digital India project and the widespread use of UPI. Not only does it foster economic growth, but it also puts people and businesses in a proactive position to leverage India's thriving digital economy.

Being the most basic mechanisms of India's digital economy, they offer safe and effective transactions that benefit consumers and companies. In that regard, they also are facilitating economic expansion and financial inclusion by encouraging independent contractors in the gig economy as well as allowing small artisans to access the national market. When it gets close, the payment gateway will remain a component of the financial system.

A mini-eshop dealing in clothing merchandise took an online payment gateway. So now with more and more payment methods added in, such as UPI and credit card options, it witnessed increase sales and revenues for its Indian business. Thus, the secure transactions because of the gateway's fraud detection mechanism could easily add confidence to these customers. Additionally, by the integration with the ecommerce stores was much easier, order processes went quite a lot more efficiently to make the shoppers enjoy this better experience.

Payment gateways are surely the backbone of online trade as they ensure security, efficiency, and reliability in modern digital transactions. This is crucial for the fast-paced, competitive economy of today. In fact, payment gateways allow any business to give their customers a seamless payment experience, which is critical to the growth of digital services, freelancing, and e-commerce in India.

Knowing how the payment gateways work and what they could do for one is of significant importance to students venturing into e-commerce or freelancing. Online stores must be set up, and international payments managed through freelancing; hence, these tools are based on which such transactions take place without any hitch or danger. Getting to know multi-currency support, fraud prevention, and platform integration allow students to master the skills on how to navigate and get the most out of digital economies.

As India continues to look into digital transformation, the role of these payment gateways will find increasing importance. They help bridge convenience but also give birth to financial inclusion and growth in the economy alongside innovations. Filling gaps through traditional banking while building that necessary trust in digital transaction, the payment gateways lay down the foundation stone of a more inclusive and powerful.

4.5.2 Case Study Example

A startup that sells handmade goods used a payment gateway and was able to reach the whole of India. However, the business faced setbacks on its first day since there was no single payment that could be used to address various customer tastes. Using a strong and efficient payment gateway, it allowed it to accept a wide variety of payment channels, which include credit/debit cards, digital wallets, and UPI, thus facilitating seamless and secure checkout processes.

This strategic move significantly widened the customer base of the startup as it allowed customers from urban areas, semi-urban, and rural regions to buy products conveniently. UPI

payments mostly catered to the niche younger and more tech-savvy customers, where including card payments attracted some traditional shoppers.More and more, it implied raising the client's confidence by providing not only increased incomes for the firm but higher security of transactions via its fraud detection capabilities of a payment gateway.

This is a perfect case where adding payment gateways helps the small business to grow in operations, satisfy its customers, and prosper in this competitive digital market.

4.6 CONCLUSION

The landscape of finance is being transformed and redefined by digital banking and payment solutions in the way people and businesses relate to money. These technologies allow users to access financial services anywhere, anytime. Features like real-time transactions, mobile payments, and online banking platforms make it easier for users to manage their finances and have empowered them for greater effectiveness in the digital economy.

Such solutions have thus been trusted because of the security and efficiency they offer, thus finding their way to both rural and urban areas. Such digital payment systems have opened up new avenues for growth for firms, especially small ones, and freelancers as well, streamlining operations and increasing markets. Similarly, to a person, these tools offer means of financial inclusion; one can get access to a bank and payment services in regions where there is no such traditional infrastructure.

With its digitization and wide adoption of banking and payment technologies in the country, India presents all of the transformative possibilities; in short, the answers are just conveniences - it's an indispensable solution to growth, innovation, and inclusion.

To face the new trends of digital economy with confidence, ease of accessibility, and assurance, people and business houses find digital banking and payments very convenient and inevitable in the integrated world.

4.7 FUTURE OF INDIA'S DIGITAL PAYMENTS

The digital payment ecosystem of India is bound to take shape significantly because of continuing innovation, supporting policies, and the infusion of advanced technology. It reflects the commitment of the nation to efficiency, technology adoption, and financial inclusion in the trajectory followed in the global digital payment ecosystem. Among the prominent events that influence the way of digital payments in India, the Digital Rupee, voice-enabled banking, and payment systems infused with IoT stand out.

Possible impacts of the digital rupee (CBDC).

The next stage that is going to revolutionize the financial sector of India is the Central Bank Digital Currency, or Digital Rupee. It is created and controlled by the Reserve Bank of India but is an RBI-regulated currency with no risk considerations similar to those of cryptocurrencies. It merges the stability and credibility of a fiat money with all the benefits of a digital currency.

Digital rupees have following advantages:

- Improved Efficiency: Digital rupee reduces the transaction cost by removing an intermediary and enhances speed of transactions with added security, which may ultimately reach people in rural areas lacking facilities of traditional banking by connection with digital channels.
- Cross-Border Trade: The Digital Rupee can facilitate smoother international trade by reducing the complexities of currency translation, thereby streamlining international payments.

Practice using the app. A small exporter in India, for example, would be able to use Digital Rupee to pay international clients instantaneously, cutting out exorbitant fees and other delays that conventional banking systems bring along with them. Thus, the opportunity of innovation might permit India to improve its external trade without letting fraudulence and non-transparency hijack it.

2. Voice banking technology and other innovations with other regional populations

One of the latest innovations intended to reach out to India's vast, diverse population, especially the semi-urban and rural populations with little or no literacy and technological exposure, is voice-enabled banking. Most first-time clients find voice-enabled systems as a barrier-free way of doing financial transactions, banking services, and commands in their mother tongue.

Features and Benefits

- Regional Language Support: More Indian languages will be supported through voice-enabled systems, which will reduce barriers for users who do not speak English.
- Usability: Users can pay bills, check their account balances, and initiate transactions by talking to their devices.
- Inclusive: The solution allows digital banking to reach older citizens and those not familiar with using mobile apps.

For example, a voice-enabled banking application can be utilized by an isolated farmer to either withdraw or check whether or not he qualifies for loan among other things. It allows the user to make the banking services customizable as simple and easy to operate as possible, in addition to financial literacy.

3. Wearables and Other Payment Services through IoT Integration

IoT is going to revolutionize digital payments in India. It is going to make transactions between connected devices seamless and contactless. That's going to redefine what simplicity in financial transactions would be, from an IoT-enabled retail setting to wearable payment devices like a fitness band and smartwatch.

Applications for IoT Payments:

- Wearables: Gadgets like smartwatches can be connected to digital wallets, so customers can make a payment with a single touch at a terminal.
- Smart Appliances: These can include appliances like fridges, voice assistants that once their supplies are low in groceries will automatically order their supply online and pay by voice commands.
- Connected Vehicles: Vehicles equipped with Internet of Things (IoT) technology may pay parking fees, petrol and tolls automatically.

Impact on Daily Life: For instance, a car may automatically pay parking costs via an app, or a commuter can pay for their coffee by just tapping their wristwatch at the counter. These technologies reduce in-person touch throughout the transaction, saving time while increasing the client experience. These solutions cut on in-person contact during transaction and therefore save time by improving the customer experience. India is on the brink of a great shift in its digital payment ecosystem. Be it the Digital Rupee or voice-enabled banking to IoT-powered payment systems, it is well placed at the forefront of innovation worldwide. Besides increasing efficiency and convenience, this would catalyze financial inclusion with millions of people being empowered and bridging the gaps between urban and rural populations. It is, therefore, important that professionals and students are well-versed about these trends to be on top of the constantly changing financial scenario. These technologies are sure to be key to a cashless, inclusive, and connected economy that will emerge from the continued digital transformation of India.

CHAPTER 5

LENDING AND CREDIT SERVICES

5.1 INTRODUCTION

Lending and credit services are one of the vital components of the world financial system, since they avail much-needed capital for growth and development among individuals, businesses, and governments. The service includes a broad range of undertakings that include, but are not limited to personal loans, business loans, mortgage loans, credit cards, among other credits. Traditionally, lending and credit services have been availed through banks and credit unions among other various financial institutions. They check the creditworthiness of the borrowers before providing loans or lines of credit by checking their credit history, income, etc. Such services enhance economic activities because they enable consumers and also the businesses concerned to manage cash flows, invest in opportunities, and realize their financial objectives.

5.1.1 Traditional Lending and Credit Systems

Traditional lending and credit systems depend on well-established financial institutions that act as intermediaries between depositors and borrowers. These systems are regulated through tough regulatory systems that always try to stabilize, make transparent, and fair financial transactions. Under the conventional model, the banks and other financial institutions use manual procedures and face-to-face interactions as a basis for creditworthiness assessments that will be used in approving loans and making repayments. The credit score of an individual depends on the centrally available databases, such as credit bureaus, that collect borrowers' history. Despite these reservations, traditional systems have remained dependable but are criticized due to several aspects including how they appear as very slow, costly, and are not accessible to underserved populations, those who are without formal credit history or the structure of traditional banking infrastructures.

5.1.2 Fintech Principles

Fintech is financial technology that innovatively revolutionized lending and credit services. Fintech uses advanced technologies such as AI, machine learning, blockchain, and big data analytics to streamline processes while reducing operational costs. The biggest examples of fintech impacting the industry are digital lending platforms, peer-to-peer, or P2P, lending, and alternative credit scoring models. The company makes use of non-traditional sources of data such as activity on social media and the history of payment to make a credit decision. That makes credit decisions faster and more accurate. Fintech makes access to credit more democratized by taking the intermediaries out of the credit system of distribution, making a solution tailored for all of these automated processes for greater audiences-small business entrepreneurs and their individual constituents locked out from the more formal systems. It is a transition that reminds the world what possible fintech can bring to lending: further inclusion to finances and economic power.

5.2 EVOLUTION OF FINTECH IN LENDING

Fintech in lending was born to revolutionize how credits are provided by bringing much-needed speed, efficiency, and accessibility to a sector that moves relatively slowly and is mainly paper-based. The term 'fintech' actually refers to the amalgamation of technology and financial services. Fintechs are known to revolutionize the lending business through various digital platforms and innovative tools, helping stream processes from application for a loan, all through credit risk assessment, then disbursement of funds. This has thus caused disruption in the model of traditional banking with an option that is more agile, customer-centric, and cost-effective. The demand for better financial inclusion and the reliance on digital solutions in the financial ecosystem drive the necessity for fintech in lending.

5.2.1 Definition and Role of Fintech in Lending

Fintech in lending refers to the use of advanced technologies to make credit provision easier and better. Fintech reduces the need for manual intervention by automating operations, bringing down operational costs significantly, and eradication of inefficiencies. These platforms allow instant loan approvals and digital documentation and provide tailored products according to every individual's need. Fintech is also critically important in bridging gaps for underbanked and unbanked populations. Through alternative credit scoring models and digital interfaces, fintech platforms offer access to credit for an individual and business entities that would not be accessed under the traditional financial system.

5.2.2 Technological Lending Advancement Artificial Intelligence and Machine Learning

Artificial Intelligence (AI) and Machine Learning (ML) have revolutionized the entire credit risk assessment process. It has made possible the automation of analysis for big data sets and predictive analytics. These technologies measure a borrower's creditworthiness based on the pattern in his financial behaviour, spending, and repayment patterns, at a level of accuracy never seen before. AI-based chatbots and virtual assistants also boost customer engagement with 24/7 support and guidance throughout the lending process.

Big Data

Fintech firms can use big data to rely on nonconventional sources of data-including utility payments, e-commerce transactions, or activity on social media-to make more savvy credit decisions. Alternative data is brought in, and consequently, there is widespread evaluation of credit risk, credit provision to individuals without formal credit history, and reduced rates of default.

Blockchain

Blockchain technology makes lending operations more transparent and secure. In blockchain, immutability of transaction records will never let fraud occur as data will be secured. Further, the smart contract reduces the complexities of lending. Loan agreement, repayment, and compliance check are carried out through automation by eradicating intermediaries.

Cloud Computing

Scalability is the infrastructure under which fintech platforms may be scaled. Lenders can deploy scalable, cost-effective solutions with solutions provided by cloud computing, enabling easy integration, real-time data processing, and high degrees of collaboration across geographies. The flexibility and resilience of cloud computing will allow for faster innovation leading to adoption of newer technologies, which will ensure that the fintech platforms are both competitive and reliable.

All these advancements altogether make fintech companies redefine lending: easy and efficient, with greater trust and transparency over financial transactions.

5.3 PEER-TO-PEER (P2P) LENDING PLATFORMS

Peer-to-Peer (P2P) lending platforms are an innovative alternative to the traditional lending systems because of the fact that these platforms connect borrowers directly to individual investors. These platforms completely eliminate the need for such intermediaries as banks, enabling direct access to the users of the loans and the return for funding the loans by investors. P2P lending typically operates through online platforms whereby borrowers publish their loan needs and investors select a loan based on the risk appetite and expected returns. Some of the most popular P2P lending platforms are LendingClub, Prosper, and Zopa, as these sites have become popularized due to easy usage and the process for loans.

5.3.1 Benefits of Peer-to-Peer Lending

P2P lending offers many benefits, and both borrowing and investment parties are attracted to its use. Compared to most traditional financial services, P2P lending has the advantage of generally lower interest rates; the elimination of middlemen reduces the operational cost. Second, these websites offer very flexible terms, which are processed quickly, so they constitute an attractive source of instantaneous funding for most individuals and small businesses.

To the investors, P2P lending offers a more elevated return than the common saving or investment products. By diversification in investments spread over multiple loans, one optimizes portfolios while balancing risk with rewards. It reduces dependence on the traditional financial intermediaries hence democratizing access to credit and investment opportunities. It fosters financial inclusion, giving more control to the participants over their lending or borrowing experience.

5.3.2 Challenges in P2P Lending

Even though P2P lending has several merits, it is still in many challenges. Amongst the major key challenges entails regulatory oversight. The regulatory environment of the P2P lending sector is relatively new with other sectors. Different regions hold significantly varied regulatory environments. The lack of a standard system of regulation has created an uncertainty of what to implement among the platform operators and borrowers as well as among investors.

Another issue is the in-built default risk inherent in lending. In the absence of financial institutions, investors will lose their money if the borrowers fail to pay back their loans. Also, P2P loans are illiquid in nature; investors are not able to sell or withdraw their investments before loan terms are completed.

While P2P lending has revolutionized access to credit and investment opportunities, it is in its best interest to address such challenges to ensure its long-term sustainability and growth in the financial landscape.

5.4 DIGITAL CREDIT SCORING SYSTEMS

Digital credit scoring systems are one of the most significant developments in the assessment of creditworthiness, using technology to enhance accuracy, inclusivity, and speed. These systems look into a more significant spectrum of data points and use advanced algorithms in delivering real-time insight into the financial behaviour of a borrower. These traditional models tend to exclude individuals without formal credit history while adopting novel methodologies that will increase the lenders' scope towards the population, promoting further financial inclusion and, eventually, underbanked individuals.

5.4.1 Traditional Credit Scoring Models

Traditionally, these models are more dependent on the information retrieved from the credit bureaus regarding the historical data in terms of payment, the amount owed, and how long the credit account has existed. Using such standardized formulae, they compute a numerical value which determines the creditworthiness of the borrower. Such models, however, come with extreme drawbacks. For individuals who do not have a conventional credit history such as young adults, freelancers, or residents in geographies with poor banking infrastructures, conventional models typically return low or null scores and therefore exclude them from access to loans or credits. Additionally, they lack the ability to adapt to new financial behaviours and, hence, make overly conservative lending decisions.

5.4.2 Emerging Trends in Credit Scoring Models

Alternative Data Sets

Alternative sources that can be used to formulate the credit scoring are of a more advanced form. It may include data of other forms, not in a traditional credit bureau. Utility payments for bills, rental histories, usage patterns of mobile phones, e-commerce activity, and even social media behaviour comprise examples of such data points. Lenders will find that the reliability of customers financially will be better known by them. Even though such borrowers will not have credit histories traditionally established in the country for example, paying electricity bills or mobile phone bills by due dates speaks very well for being financially responsible and the such underbanked customers will also qualify for credit.

Machine Learning End

The new millennium has seen the significance of machine learning in modern day credit scoring as the concept can provide dynamic as well as personalized models. These algorithms work in real-time on large data sets, thereby revealing patterns and trends that a static model would not be able to detect. Because this process is based on machine learning, the scoring system is adaptive, meaning it can get better at its accuracy with every new data availability. Different variables might be used while making the system adaptive. These include changes in the pattern of income and expenditure behaviour as well as other economic patterns. This helps in giving a fine, personalized assessment of credit risk, which is more effective than the traditional methods in both terms of predictive ability and inherent bias-reduction.

With these advanced approaches, the digital credit scoring system brings more equitable and efficient credit to lenders who can then make decisions based on facts while extending access to credit to previously underserved populations.

5.5 ONLINE LENDING PLATFORMS

Online lending platforms are digital solutions that provide end-to-end loan services over the internet, doing away with the need for traditional bank branches or physical paperwork. This avenue brings an application of technology to make lending simple from loan application up to disbursement and until full repayment. Thus, the whole idea reduces the intermediary role that would otherwise be played by the banks. Online lending has been streamlined while operations and costs have declined with more convenient and prompt access for borrowers and also for lenders. Their digital nature makes access to loans rather speedy, which often necessitates only minimal documentation and highly automated decision-making based on advanced algorithms and data analytics. These platforms can be designed to integrate with various industries such as e-commerce, healthcare, or education, leading to finance products offering services to these specific sectors tailored to their needs and individualized requirements within such fields.

Online lending platforms are in huge demand as they are so convenient to use, friendly in their interface, and agile. They can range from access to personal loans for individuals to working capitals or start-up fund acquisition for small businesses. Frequently, such platforms make use of alternative data and advance credit-scoring models for determining the creditworthiness of an applicant. Sometimes, it might be the case that someone without formal or limited credit history still finds a loan. Mobile applications and interfaces complement this feature to give convenience and access to people from different parts of the country in getting these loaning services, and an Internet connection allows them to request for loans and oversee finances anywhere.

Examples and Applications

Some of the popular online lending services that have come up and have been involved with several types of service rendered, focusing on one part of the borrowers than the other are:

This one falls in the topmost preferred online lending websites that specialize in providing products such as personal loans, student loan refinancing options, refinanced mortgages, etc. Based on technology, **SoFi** acts as an intermediary entity for helping provide better terms and faster acceptance to its borrower compared with traditional ones. It is also serving its users in investment, as well as wealth management.

Upstart: Using machine learning and artificial intelligence, Upstart is lending personal loans to those people who do not have proper credit. Today it is possible to lend money to those people whose credentials would have been refused through the usual channels of lending due to other forms of data such as education and their work history, etc.

Kabbage: Kabbage is the fintech company that specializes in providing small business loans. The company has direct access to the financial accounts of the owners and makes real-time decisions concerning the health of a business's money, offering fast, auto-funded funding. This system avails businesses with more easy and paperless access to capital than loans from most traditional banks.

Use Cases

Online lending platforms cater to numerous demands for finance and are used in numerous industries.

Personal Loans: These platforms offer personal loans for other purposes also, such as debt consolidation, improving homes, and so on. Here, the biggest attraction is toward such platforms is the need of those borrowers who require easy, flexible, and fast access to financial solutions.

Business Financing: Most small businesses and start-ups these days borrow business loans and lines of credit through online lending platforms. Loans can help small businesses handle working capital, cash flow, and expand the businesses. Kabbage may provide much faster and accessible financing than bank loans by utilizing alternative data and machine learning models.

Online Lending for Student Loans SoFi is an online lending site specialized in the refinancing and student loans. This makes it easy for students to acquire funds for educational purposes and to refinance student debt at discounted rates. The online lending method of student loans is quicker with superior, more tailored repayment programs.

Besides that, there are other e-commerce, health-related, and education service companies providing online lending services. For example, at the point of sale, the e-commerce can easily offer loans or financing for high-value commodities that the consumers are purchasing. Healthcare companies can also partner with online lenders since the latter offers financing programs for health services. In the same way, educational institutions can partner with online lending companies and provide low-interest loans to customers for tuition or professional development.

With constant exposure to various consumer and business financial needs, the online lending sites continue shaping the face of lending so that credit is accessible, efficient, and targeted appropriately in different circumstances.

5.6 LOAN MANAGEMENT SOFTWARE

LMS, or loan management software, is an integrated platform that automates the entire loan lifecycle, beginning with origination through servicing and monitoring. These systems integrate various functions associated with loan processing, including application management, credit risk assessment, disbursement, repayment tracking, and collections. All these activities will be centralized in one system, thus improving the efficiency of financial institutions while at the same time enhancing customer experience through faster and more accurate services while reducing the administrative burden associated with the manual processing. Now, most of the modern LMS solutions have some feature or other like real-time tracking, customized reporting, compliance management, etc. They enable lenders to keep easy records and up-to-date with all the requirements so that borrowers can have a better experience.

The business is made streamlined by loan management software because many of its key processes of this lending industry get automated for the purpose of making the process highly efficient and accurate in its approach. One of its significant features is loan origination automation, which helps streamline both application processes and approval processes as it reduces manual paperwork along with accelerating a decision-making process. Additionally, these platforms also provide real-time loan servicing; so, it updates loan data as there are repayments, and it tries to avoid mistakes in terms of account management. Moreover, the software consists of monitoring tools that outline outstanding balances, due dates, and payment statuses, through which lenders may take proactive action if needed. Customizable reporting features allow lenders to generate detailed financial reports, monitor portfolio performance, and track key metrics such as delinquencies and defaults. Second, most loan management systems provide compliance management tools to keep up with all the different regulations whether local or international, like Know Your Customer and Anti-Money Laundering which reduce the risks of sanctions legally or regulatory.

Examples

Some of the best loan management software include nCino, LendingTree, and Finastra.

nCino is a cloud-based banking platform that allows the management of end-to-end loan origination and management. It helps banks and credit unions streamline the loan process from application, through underwriting and closing, and integrates with their existing core banking systems. nCino is very popular due to its friendly interface and seamless integration with Salesforce.

LendingTree is more of a known online marketplace. It connects consumers to several lenders, and it may offer comparison tools for a broad range of loan products, but LendingTree's loan management platform also supports lenders in the efficient tracking, managing, and processing of loan applications coming through different channels and has helped reduce operational inefficiencies for better customer engagement.

Finastra features a whole suite of lending products that, as reported to be, it has loan origination servicing and tools for risk management. The software supported the wide range of personal loans, business loans, and mortgages. What this solution does is assist in enhancing financial service delivery, automating processes, and effectively and efficiently managing portfolios.

5.6.1 Implication to Efficiency

Loan management software is the one that significantly impacts the efficiency of lending operations. The saving of time and the reduction of human error by automating tasks such as loan origination, underwriting, and repayment tracking can make financial institutions process more loans in a short time and therefore save costs. Automated compliance management also saves financial institutions from costly non-compliance fines and the implications thereof in court.

This then also translates to a better user experience for both lenders and borrowers. In the case of the lenders, automation of tasks which were manually operated then allows them to make quicker decisions with a better workflow, enabling them to serve more clients using fewer resources. The loan management platform allows for approval much more rapidly and provides easier access to account information and real-time updates of loan status. This typically makes the borrowing process clear and easier for the borrowers. One can help improve timely updates and personalized service offerings to increase customer satisfaction and loyalty with business growth.

Summary With all that loan management software does by making some of the most important processes automated, thus cutting costs of operations in place, increasing benefits toward lending and borrowing parties, thereby helping lenders become more competitive in creating better financial inclusion and customer engagement with maximum efficiency.

5.7 FRAMEWORK OF REGULATION

The regulation of lending in fintech is changing fast because governments and regulatory bodies around the world are trying to come up with laws and guidelines meant to govern the functioning of the fintech platforms. Such regulations look for a balanced expression between the innovation of the financial sector and the protection of consumers, maintenance of finance stability, and development of integrity in the market. As fintech lending expands across the world, so does the regulatory bodies grow with them. They evolve according to the new digital platform and issues revolving around privacy and security of data, cross border lending, and issues of fraud.

5.7.1 Global Regulatory Landscape

Laws governing a fintech lending platform differ from one region to another, which simply speaks to legal and cultural environments where the operation is conducted. General financial services regulation applies to fintech lending in most countries on the one hand, while specific regulations relating to technology, digital platforms, and data protection govern the same on the other. For instance, the European Union has the General Data Protection Regulation that defines the method of collection, processing, and storage of personal data, which will therefore influence the manner in which fintech lenders operate within the EU. This is also in line with the United States, where California's Consumer Privacy Act (CCPA) establishes consumer rights when it comes to collection and privacy of data. Fintech lenders must ensure that they operate in accordance with these laws, which may not only differ by country but even by regions within the same country. Thus, they must employ stringent security measures to protect the sensitive data of borrowers and treat consumer rights with dignity at each juncture in lending.

Data Protection Laws: Following strict data protection laws such as GDPR and CCPA, a fintech lending platform will have to take into consideration the rights of an individual in terms of how to safeguard his/her personal information and to be transparent about how this data is going to be used. These laws require that strict measures must be applied in collecting, processing, storing, and sharing data, along with consent from the consumer. They also have to have explicit disclosures on the use of consumer data and allow consumers to access, correct, or delete their data. Severe penalties occur if non-compliance is made with such regulations, thus making compliance critical for fintech lenders as it integrates a very essential framework in their operation systems. In addition, changes of data protection regulations have the effect of creating difficulties that lenders face in staying current and keeping up-to-date compliance across several jurisdictions.

5.7.2 Regulatory Challenges

Regulatory Complexities of Cross-Border Lending

Some of the largest challenges in the governance of fintech lending sites have been the cross-country characteristics of most digital institutions. While some fintech financiers limited their operations to specified nations, others have increased going worldwide offering services to client's border to border. There come complex issues brought by exceptional legal and regulatory frameworks related to each jurisdiction with different compliance issues increasing by varied regions. For example, in this case, the U.S.-based fintech lenders would still fall within the purview of GDPR even if they do operate outside the EU. The grounds for this are based on the fact that the data protection law applies anywhere when it is relevant within the territory. This would indeed be adding complexity to their business processes and make it more cumbersome for fintech lenders to have local entities or partnerships for establishing the same.

5.7.3 The Balance Between Innovation and Consumer Protection Challenge: Tipping the Balance

The striking of a balance between innovation and consumer protection remains another challenge since regulators will be required to encourage innovations related to new lending technologies and business models as well as safeguards against risks such as fraud, predatory lending, and data misuse. This is a challenge of ensuring as much flexibility to fintech companies to innovate but, at the same time, protecting consumers from worse attitudes.

Over-regulation will suppress innovation, and lack of regulation will provide scopes for exploitation and erode consumer trust.

5.7.4 Sandbox Environments

To address this challenge, most governments have established sandbox environments where fintech companies will be allowed to conduct new lending solutions and technologies under controlled and regulated spaces. Generally speaking, regulatory sandboxes exist with the view of innovative operations while guaranteeing full observance of consumer rights as well as regulatory conditions. These usually provide waived fintech companies employing live customer experimentation of newly developed financial product and service but staying within a regime that ensures effective risk control and observatory measures. One example of such is the well-known sandbox of the UK Financial Conduct Authority (FCA). The sandbox allows the testing of fintech products live in the market while satisfying all extant legislation. Sandbox initiatives are able to help the regulators learn better about the emerging technology and market trends, making it possible for the innovators to scale their product in a controlled environment which is safe for them as well.

In summary, there is a very complex regulatory environment for lending through fintech, where there is this constant fight globally in attempts to try and keep abreast of the new technological waves while at the same time keeping the citizens protected and maintaining stability in the financial system. The future of fintech lending will include cross border issues, mandates of data protection, the demand of regulatory sandboxes, amongst others, meaning there is an ever more urgent need for cooperation across regulators, fintech lenders, and the customers.

5.8 CHALLENGES IN FINTECH LENDING

Leveraging fintech lending is an important step forward in making accessibility, speed, and efficiency come together for the lending domain. It does, however, throw up a new set of unprecedented challenges which need to be addressed for fintech lenders to build trust, continue to maintain operational integrity, and ensure long-term success: data security and privacy and default and fraud risks - and scalability and sustainability, among others.

Data Security and Privacy

One of the biggest risks to fintech lending is robust data security and protection of privacy. Fintech platforms are highly susceptible to cyber-attacks, data breaches, and identity theft because they process and store large amounts of sensitive financial information on their platforms. In the event of successful penetration, apart from the risk of losing money belonging to customers or lenders, it may also harm the reputation of the lending platform and damage consumers' confidence. With each new step in terms of technologies- AI and machine learning-this threat grows. They expand the list of services with enhanced cybersecurity features, and the process gets even more complicated.

What is significant here is protecting the trust of digital customers. The consumers need to feel sure that all of their private information, financial information as well as the entirety of their transactions are protected against unauthorized access. To achieve this kind of effort, fintech companies have to spend money in high-tech security measures including end-to-end encryption, multi-factor authentication, and international privacy regulations such as GDPR and CCPA. Such security protocols not only minimize the risks of cyber threats but also build trust and credibility within the fintech lending ecosystem. Default and Fraud Risks

Another challenge in fintech lending is to manage default and fraud risks. Many persons and businesses to whom a lending fintech advances credits have not developed comprehensive or traditional credit history, so there is a higher probability of default and fraud. Alternative data could be a boon to the credit scoring model but creates hard-to-handle issues while gauging the credibility of such borrowers who appear opaque or seem to have irregular finances.

Digital lending fraud encompasses, but is not limited to, identity theft and loan stacking, where a borrower takes out multiple loans from different lenders without the knowledge of others. This is about fraudsters exploiting weaknesses in the application or verification process to gain unauthorized access to funds. Fintech platforms face the biggest challenge in balancing efficient loan processing with risk mitigation strategies.

Advanced systems must be in place by fintech lenders that can identify fraudulent patterns and behaviours. AI-based algorithms would detect unusual patterns and behaviour by the borrowers. Machine learning will enable lenders to judge the probability of fraud against a borrower's digital footprint, such as an abnormal activity in social media or inconsistent online activities. Better verification techniques would be employed to prevent fraud, like biometric authentication.

Scalability and Sustainability

As fintech lending platforms grow, scalability and sustainability emerge as issues. Scaling of such growth usually requires tremendous volumes of transactions, customers, and data, which in turn overwhelm current systems and infrastructure. Ensuring such a platform scales without causing degradation in performance, security, or customer experience becomes critical. Operational inefficiency and customer dissatisfaction might happen if not scaled correctly along with system outages.

Fintech companies need to be sustainable through their business models. Growth brings the challenge of maintaining the balance between aggressive growth and operation efficiency to their business models. Scalable operation is required by fintech lenders through investments in cloud computing, automation, and modular technologies. Well-architected platform will ensure that when there are increased users, the platform will also be responsive and efficient enough.

Moreover, in long-term sustainability, risk management building a strong framework is involved: immunity to market fluctuation and change in regulatory policies. Fintech lenders should maintain continuous and adaptive vigilance regarding developments in economic circumstances, consumer behaviour, and regulatory conditions to ensure that their business models remain resistant. By focusing on sustainable practices-from responsible lending, financial inclusion, and compliance-the platform will firmly put itself into a position to stand the test of long-run success and away from short-term growth tactics that are neither scalable nor ethical.

In a nutshell, the idea of fintech lending can be revolutionary, but issues of data security and fraud prevention and sustainability raise major concerns. These challenges can be better addressed by regulations that are strong, comply with modern technological advancement, and business practices that engender confidence and mitigate risk for sustainable growth in the fintech lending platforms.

5.9 FUTURE TRENDS IN LENDING AND CREDIT SERVICES

The landscape of lending and credit services is changing at a fast pace with the advancement of technology, changes in consumer preferences, and regulatory developments. As the financial ecosystem becomes increasingly digital, several key trends shape the future of lending. These trends reflect the growing influence of technological innovation and highlight a shift toward more personalized, inclusive, and sustainable lending practices.

AI-Driven Lending Decisions

AI-driven lending decisions are fast becoming the new favourite among financial institutions as they look to make the accuracy, speed, and fairness of their credit assessments better and more workable. The largest trends here include the adoption of what's known as **explainable AI, or XAI**, which guarantees that AI-driven decisions are going to be transparent and easy to understand for the borrowing individuals and for the regulators. Unlike the traditional models, which normally act as "black boxes," explainable AI provides very clear reasoning behind loan approval or denial. It means that it provides better explanations of why a decision is made thus helping the borrower address his concern about bias and discrimination thereby making AI fair and equitable. For the lenders, AI-based decision-making would mean more accurate risk appraisal and faster loan disbursal with higher prospects of fewer defaults and an overall better process. In addition, AI enables personalization of loan offerings by making extensive data analysis for custom terms to a borrower's unique financial profile.

Embedded Finance

One of the new trends coming under this area is that of embedded finance. This deals directly with the integration of services, such as lending, with non-financial platforms and applications that consumers already use in order to run their daily affairs. After all, one can observe this most vividly in the form of **Buy Now, Pay Later (BNPL) services**, where consumers receive credit instantly at the moment of purchase via e-commerce platforms or retail apps. While going through the checkout, the consumers will finance purchases more readily in smaller instalments that might be manageable, with the providers like Klarna and Afterpay working with the retailers to offer credit in a seamless manner. However, outside of BNPL, this embedded finance also offers other lending solutions that could be integrated into ride-sharing applications, payment platforms, even social media. This shift may, therefore, exponentially increase the access to credit especially for the young and savvy population who may not engage with the banks in conventional ways. Embedded finance clears up borrowing process and enables access at any and all points of a need saving time by slicing out all the barriers associated with financial institutions.

Decentralized Finance (DeFi)

Decentralized Finance is an evolution change in lending and delivering credit services. DeFi uses blockchain to exchange peer-to-peer (P2P) lending and borrowing without central intermediaries, such as banks or credit unions. Smart contracts on blockchain sites like Ethereum help remove central authorities, allowing access to transactions at a more decentralized level, which may lower some fees. Besides, DeFi might lead to flexible and accessible financial products. For this, any internet user is able to become a lender or borrow irrespective of more traditional systems of banking. All that creates a whole vista of financial inclusion into formerly unreached underserved or altogether unbanked populations. The second is that DeFi accommodates more personal loan terms, for example, interest rates and repayment schedules as determined by the relationship of the borrower and lender and not by authority or any central decision. However, DeFi is in a very nascent stage and needs to overcome many regulatory challenges and sustainability for it to achieve mainstream adoption.

Lending Sustainability

As the environmental issue becomes visible to everyone living on earth, it goes on mounting pressure from **different financial institutions** to make sure that their lending policies encourage sustainable initiatives. **Green loans** happen to be one among evolving finance that targets and goes for environmentally friendly financing for projects. Generally, the lending service provides favourable terms and conditions to the borrowers as they invest in energy efficient technologies, renewable energy-based projects, or other sustainability activities. More lenders are now including environmental, social, and governance factors in their credit analyses in order to identify a borrower's business strategy in line with the sustainability of goals apart from green loans. It forms part of a gigantic movement towards sustainable finance that is the direction where the financial institutions aggressively are proposing an initiative reducing carbon footprint, building social equity, and strengthening long-term environmental stewardship. Banks, for instance can offer reduced interest rates to projects with a reduction in carbon emissions, while investing into clean energy research and development. Increasingly, lending is becoming sustainable, and it represents the consumer's demand for ethical investments, along with recognition that financial services greatly drive positive social and environmental change.

In summary, the future of lending and credit services is going to be technologically deep, more inclusive, and far more transparent. The scenarios of smarter lending decisions more individualized will be empowered by AI. Embedded finance and decentralized finance, on the other hand, will make financial services available and less dependent on traditional intermediaries. The fact makes the sustainable push by the financial institutes towards both environmental and social projects and lending push it to become a high power mechanism for positive transformation at a global scale. Last but not the least, unprecedented change comes in the form of financial services where technologies are integrated within lending and credits that transform the whole cycle into inclusive, efficient, and more customer-centric. Traditional lending models, often plagued by rigid structures and very limited access to financial services, are being transformed. Advances such as AI, ML, big data analytics, blockchain, and cloud computing powering fintech innovations have transformed the credit decisioning and loan management approach and interfaces between the borrowers and the lenders in many profound ways. In so far as fintech not only makes financial services accessible but also fast tracks the processing of credit with a faster and more precise approach to assessing credit, then such would surely make for a more agile and responsive financial environment.

It also has the ability to democratize access to credit because it gives a solution to those who had previously been underserved or excluded from traditional banking systems. Fintech is increasing financial inclusion through alternative credit scoring models, peer-to-peer lending platforms, and digital wallets that enable people who reside in remote villages or have no credit history to be loaned. However, in this transformation comes a whole new set of challenges - more particularly in the forms of data privacy and security, coupled with the need for effective regulatory frameworks to keep up with innovation while being protective towards consumers. In summary, fintech is changing lending and credit provision but also removes the long-standing barriers to access financial services and thus making it possible for individuals and firms to thrive within a more digital economy.

5.10 IMPACT OF FINTECH ON LENDING ACCESSIBILITY FOR THE UNDERBANKED

Fintech has improved lending accessibility to the underbanked by developing solutions that circumvent traditional banking infrastructure. For example, digital lending and mobile banking applications provide distant people with the facility of applying for a loan without ever visiting a bank. Fintech companies assess their creditworthiness using sources that are diversified into mobile phone usage, utility payments, and social media activities. That's very useful for the population that lacks formal credit history or gains proper access to traditional sources of financial services. P2P lending platforms directly link the borrowers with lenders. They do not have any middlemen; therefore, the cost of credit comes down. Thus, credit becomes cheaper and is made available to those who could not be included in the financial system.

Role of Machine Learning in Modern Credit Scoring Systems

The most important role that machine learning holds in today's credit score systems is that it enables much more dynamic, personable, and accurate levels of assessment about creditworthiness. The traditional credit-scoring system primarily relies upon static factors, which happen to be credit history and debt-to-income ratio. Machine learning models, conversely, can analyze such a huge amount of data, including alternative data, such as payment histories in rent, utilities, and mobile phones, as well as such dynamic factors as spending patterns. These models work on algorithms that will learn vast datasets of patterns and trends that even human analysts might miss. This thus implies that the machine learning scoring systems are able to provide better in the insight in financial practice of a borrower and likely to result in a fair, more equitable, and larger number of credit decisions. Also, the models are able to adapt therefore finer as time goes on and having an enhanced predictive capability, since data become accumulated.

Advantages and disadvantages of peer-to-peer lending platforms.

The following benefits to the borrower and lender can be provided by a P2P lending platform, which is capital. P2P lending has been found as an alternative source for those borrowers who would have otherwise had stiff requirements from banks that would have approved their loans. They provide opportunities to people and businesses that were rejected by banks due to having very limited credit history or financial profiles beyond the norms. P2P lending allows the lenders to earn competitive returns on investment while still letting the lenders choose the amount of risk they are willing to take.

However, P2P lending also has some very significant challenges. Some of the most important amongst these are that it lacks regulation oversight as compared to traditional banks, which exposes both lenders and borrowers to risks like fraud, default, or even mismanagement. However, when assessing creditworthiness, a P2P lending platform is still able to access large amounts of data and may use traditional scoring methods or alternative data sources that may not necessarily reflect the financial situation of all the borrowers. Another challenge which could result is the bankruptcy of the platform; when the platform goes bankrupt, the investor will lose his money. Finally, P2P lending democratizes access to credit, but not free from scepticism. Most consumers may be unaware of the entire online lending process and also wary of the platform's risk management.

CHAPTER 6

INVESTMENT AND WEALTH MANAGEMENT IN FINTECH

6.1 INTRODUCTION TO INVESTMENT AND WEALTH MANAGEMENT

Investment and wealth management is the strategic process of management of financial resources of an individual or an organization to bring about certain financial goals and objectives. Such services include investment planning, asset allocation, tax planning, and risk management and estate planning, among others. Therefore, wealth management is defined as a holistic approach that integrates financial planning with investment advisory services specifically tailored to the needs of certain clients. The base purpose is to grow and conserve and optimize wealth into building long-term financial safety and security. With all these changes in the monetary market and with the emergence of digital technology, investment as well as wealth management undergo radical changes and integrate older traditions with newer fintech technologies.

6.1.1 Definition of Wealth Management

It can be simply said that Wealth Management is a holistic and total service that covers an individual's entire financial world. Unlike investment services, financial advisory may be narrow-minded as far as specialties go, focusing just on investments. Wealth management encompasses a broader range that will provide a strategy and blueprint to build and accumulate wealth in a no-risk financial environment. One program may encompass investment management, retirement planning, estate planning, and insurance. Usually, the core services are to create a customized focus of a high net worth individual, family, or company that would require customized asset management techniques.

6.1.2 TRADITIONAL INVESTMENT APPROACHES VS FINTECH REVOLUTION

Traditional investment approaches are based on manual processes with human expertise, and clients have to rely on advice from financial advisers or brokers for making the right investment decisions. Such methods work mainly upon historical data, few risk tolerance assessments, and some general financial models to draw investment decisions. Being effective in their own right, traditional approaches are often considered lengthy, expensive, and less accessible to minor investors.

The disruption in the traditional methods was done through the aid of a digital platform, with robo-advisors and an algorithm-driven tool as a key driver for fintech. For example, with advanced algorithms, such robo-advisors can actually be tailored so that users receive investment advice and view the automatic changes in one's portfolio while rebalancing it through these self-serviced platforms as compared to some expensive fees paid for large investors on such services. Additionally, fintech solutions use real-time data analytics, machine learning, and blockchain technology to provide better transparency, improve decision-making, and reduce risks. Fintech-driven methods are now replacing traditional ones because they have opened access to investment services, made it more inclusive, efficient, and scalable.

6.1.3 INFLUENCE OF TECHNOLOGY ON INVESTMENT STRATEGY

Technology has profoundly changed investment strategies to the extent that it has supported a data-driven, real-time, and more personified approach to wealth management. Big data analytics combined with artificial intelligence enables these wealth managers to analyze tons of financial data, creating trends and opportunities that underpin more strategic investment decisions. Machine learning models predict market movements based on changing conditions and are optimized to enhance returns on investments while managing risks at the same time.

New technology brings new possibilities such as tokenized assets and decentralized finance avenues through which investors can create their wealth.

All these innovations make the environment open and transparent, secure along with facilitating access to large assets such as real estate and commodities and cryptocurrencies.

Thanks to cloud computing and mobile technology, the client can so easily check his portfolio at any given time through investment platforms. With personalized apps and tools, the investor has control and command over his financial future, while real-time feedback and monitoring go a long way towards the whole change of strategy regarding investment, thus forming new all-inclusive apt strategies suited to the latest needs of the modern-day investor

6.2 INVESTMENT MODELS FOR THE CONVENTIONAL PAST

Traditional investment models have been the backbone of managing one's financial resources for so long; it is actually simplified to personal consulting, established investment products, and the balance between risk and return. These models revolve around human expertise that places decisions on investments where such investments are tailored fit according to the individual's own financial needs and goals. In a world where financial solutions are surrounded by all kinds of technology, a personal service and proven methods mean that traditional models find ways to survive.

6.2.1 Overview of Traditional Wealth Management

Traditional wealth management holds a whole spectrum of financial services that touch every part of a client's life. The services include asset growth strategy, risk protection, tax efficiency, and estate planning. Fintech doesn't believe in standard solutions like traditional wealth management. They rely instead on the personal relations between their clients and their advisors. For instance, an advisor needs to consult with clients so that their investment can mirror their aims, risks tolerance, and life.

Traditional wealth management generally relies on theories well established in the financial literature, like Modern Portfolio Theory, for the optimal allocation and diversification of assets. In general, the balanced portfolio between growth and stability would involve a combination of cash, bonds, and other asset classes. A high net worth or many complex financial needs require a traditional wealth management service. Financial Advisor

6.2.2 Financial advisors are the pillars of old models of investment.

They will give expert advice to overcome the complexity of financial planning and investment management. Some of their roles include the following:

- **Personalized Planning:** Advisors assess each client's financial situation, including income, expenses, assets, and liabilities, to come up with a customized plan for investment.
- **Ongoing Support:** Advisors keep abreast of market conditions and monitor client portfolios and adjust these portfolios according to the shifting goals or trends in the market.
- **Risk Management:** They guide clients to understand and manage the risks of investment, making sure that portfolios match their risk tolerance.
- **Education:** They educate clients about the principles of investment to make informed decisions.

In other words, trust and long-term relationships, as created by the human factor in financial advice, have been absent in most of the automated investment platforms. Advisors also help the investors to cope with market fluctuation and maintain focus toward long-term goals.

6.2.3 Mutual Funds, ETFs and Other Traditional Investment Vehicles

Traditional investment models use fully developed financial instruments to assemble diversified portfolios. Few major investment mediums are:

- **Mutual Funds:** Aggregate funds managed professionally distribute the pool money in class of investment. Mutual Funds provide diversification and easy access mechanisms along with professional management and thus form one of the favourites among the individual investor.
- **Exchange Traded Funds (ETFs):** The same like Mutual Funds, but are traded at the Stock Exchange and can combine all the diversified advantage of mutual fund by a liquidity like that of Stocks. Quite often cheap, and quite flexible as well.
- **Bonds:** These are fixed income securities which provide a regular flow of income. Bonds help to reduce portfolio risk and also preserve the capital.
- **Stocks:** Equities represent ownership in companies and carry the potential for growth. Traditional models emphasize selecting individual stocks through their fundamental analysis.
- **REITs:** REITs allow investors to own real estate without actually owning physical property. They provide diversification and income.

These are vehicle selections based on the client's financial objectives, time horizon, and risk capacity to ascertain that portfolios are tailored specifically to meet their needs.

Risk and Return Calculations in Traditional Investments

Risk and return form the core of traditional investment strategies, as they provide the framework to build portfolios and make asset allocations. To measure risk, financial planners use quantitative measurements such as:
Standard Deviation: This measures the volatility of investment returns.

Beta: This measures the sensitivity of an asset to market movement.

Sharpe Ratio: Measures the risk-adjusted returns.

6.3 TECHNOLOGY ADVANCEMENTS IN WEALTH MANAGEMENT

Dramatic changes in wealth management today result from the integration of the leading-edge technologies that can enhance investment strategies, reduce efficiency, and personalize services for clients. Emerging technologies, including AI and machine learning, robo-advisors, blockchain and cryptocurrencies, and big data and analytics, redefine the playing field and create new horizons for investors and professionals in wealth management.

6.3.1 AI and Machine Learning in Wealth Management

Artificial Intelligence (AI) and Machine Learning (ML) have transformed the face of wealth management where decisions get smarter and highly personalized to clients. In these systems, routine works are auto-processed along with optimized investment strategies; risk is also managed because AI algorithms process vast information that human advisors may not view, so predictive analytics comes into being that can help predict the market trends or asset performance. The machine learning algorithms learn from historical data constantly and adjust the portfolio strategy to develop highly customized investment plans. AI systems further support portfolio optimization by discovering and mitigating risks in real time, thereby always keeping clients' portfolios in line with their financial objectives. Further, AI applications in wealth management can also provide better client experiences by allowing personalized advice, automated routine inquiries through chatbots, and predicting client needs using behavioral data.

6.3.2 Robo-Advisors: The New Wave of Algorithm-Driven Investments

The robo-advisors have been a significant innovation in the delivery of wealth management services. Since algorithms are used to design and monitor investment portfolios for robo-advisors, this service is easy and less expensive for clients than traditional financial advisory services. Since robo-advisors analyze a client's financial situation, risk tolerance, and his investment goals based on advanced algorithms, they provide recommendations for a personalization of investment portfolios. Another advantage robo-advisors offer is cost-effective investment management services offerings usually lower fees than for which human advisors charge, though they are convenient, giving their clients access to manage their portfolios online in accordance with their wills and fancies. Companies like Betterment and Wealthfront have been at the forefront of robo-advisory services as effective means of servicing clients that range from retail investors through more affluent individuals. Indeed, despite some challenges-considerations of regulatory restrictions and market volatility-robo-advisors continue gaining ground because they can actually make wealth management easier, lowering the barrier to a wider range of investors.

6.3.3 Blockchain and Cryptocurrencies in Investment Strategy

Blockchain technology and cryptocurrencies are fundamentally new in terms of the approach one makes towards investments, besides opening new asset classes and bringing in secure and transparent forms of transactions. Blockchain serves as a decentralized ledger-based system that does away with intermediaries, ensuring such transactions are transparent and are also secure. This automatically reduces the risk of fraudulent transactions but also improves operational efficiency in financial operations through transferring assets and recording trade. Cryptocurrencies, such as Bitcoin and Ethereum, are an example of high growth potential but also of risk and volatility; therefore, it is a good addition but speculative for portfolios. Additionally, blockchain tokenization allows for fractional ownership and thus even better liquidity in what are otherwise classic assets that include real estate, art, or even collectibles. With its further development, blockchain might be quite an integral constituent of various investment strategies which will create a diversified portfolio and open even more channels to invest. Although there are regulatory issues and volatility in the market, it is an area of significant interest for wealth management professionals who want to innovate and grow.

6.3.4 Big Data and Analytics for Personalized Investment Advice

Big data and advanced analytics are revolutionizing the face of wealth management by giving wealth managers far deeper insights into client behaviour, market trends, and investment opportunities. The ability to analyze large volumes of data from various sources, such as market movements, social media sentiment, and economic indicators, allows wealth managers to offer more tailored advice. Big data tools can even predict the performance of assets, identify trends in emerging markets, and even predict a client's future investment preferences using predictive analytics. And big data allows wealth managers to get a much granular understanding of client profiles in order to create more personal investment strategies that align better with the individual's goal, risk tolerance, and timelines. This data-driven approach also enables wealth managers to prove themselves with a more correct piece of investment advice, at the same time deepening relationships with clients. Finally, this real-time access allows them to alter course strategies based on market behaviour at short notice, which ensures greater agility and responsiveness by their clients in the sphere of wealth management.

This is due to fast integration of AI, robo-advisors, blockchain, and big data in the wealth management industry for making services for investors more accessible, efficient, and personalized. In this regard, wealth managers will face a challenge by the progressing technologies, specifically with regard to competitiveness and increased demand for innovative, data-driven investment solutions. Already, these new advancements promise and transform wealth management in becoming more transparent, client-centric, and responsive to the changing dynamics of finance.

6.4 ROBO-ADVISORS: REINVENTING WEALTH MANAGEMENT

Robo-advisors change the face of wealth management as they make automation and algorithm-driven investment management for clients. Through the digital platforms, it applies complex algorithms in ascertaining the financial status, risk capacity, and goals of the client before presenting a customized investment portfolio. Technology-based, robo-advisors give low-cost, highly accessible alternative to traditional financial advisory services. They are primarily used by the young investor or one with smaller portfolios as they may not be able to access the traditional wealth management services primarily due to costs and high minimum investment threshold.

6.4.1 What Are Robo-Advisors?

Robo-advisors are computerized platforms through which the investor gets his or her financial planning and investment advisory service provided algorithmically on a systematic basis. They use technology to analyze the risk profile, goals, and individual client preferences to design customized investment plans without human intervention. Unlike traditional wealth managers, robo-advisors use mathematical algorithms and data analysis to make investment decisions and management. They often have several low-cost investment options like index funds and ETFs. These are designed to reflect the risk profile and financial objectives of each client. Robo-advisors democratize wealth management by making investment services accessible to individuals who have little wealth or cannot afford to pay for a professional advisor.

6.4.2 How Robo-Advisors Work: Algorithms and Risk Profiling

Robo-advisors rely on sophisticated algorithms to guide their investment decisions. The process of robo-advisory starts with a client answering an online questionnaire that evaluates the customer's financial status, investment objectives, and risk appetite. Therefore, this individualized portfolio, which is a typical mix of a diversified basket of low-cost index funds or ETFs, will be produced by the robo-advisor. Then, the algorithms, based on modern portfolio theory, will design the best possible allocation strategy in a way that it would result in a good balance between risk and return and well fits the client's profile.

Robo-advisors also continuously monitor and rebalance the portfolios so that they are always in line with the clients' shifting financial goals. Some even use more sophisticated machine learning algorithms to provide even more personalized investment solutions, constantly changing the strategy based on real-time changes in data and the situation in the markets. Most robo-advisors will also give the client tax optimization techniques, such as tax-loss harvesting, to minimize tax liabilities.

6.4.3 Advantage Over Other Wealth Management Services

Robo-advisors are distinct from other traditional wealth management services with the following critical advantages:

Cost-Efficiency: It is considerably cheaper for the client in comparison to hiring traditional financial advisors. Their fee range is at 0.25% to 0.50% for assets under management, as compared to the usual 1% or higher charged by a traditional advisor.

Accessibility: It means that robo-advisors are online; thereby, clients can gain investment management services at any point in time from any accessible location. In that sense, accessibility of wealth management services is widened by greater populations, for instance younger investors and individuals who possess minimum knowledge about investments.

Personalization at Scale: Algorithmically, robos can generate high levels of personalization very speedily given a range of factors including one's objectives, risk, and horizon. Traditionally, such personalization would not come within the purview of smaller portfolio advice.

Automation and Efficiency: Ro-bo-advisors automated the process of investing, portfolio rebalancing and tax-loss harvesting, and hence make asset management a more efficient activity with the least or no human interaction. Chances of humans making mistakes and improvement of operational efficiency due to automation

6.4.4 Regulatory landscape and challenges

While robo-advisors offer numerous benefits, they also face several regulatory and operational challenges that could impact their future growth and development.

Regulatory Oversight: Robo-advisors are regulated at the same level as an old-fashioned financial advisor. This includes, in the United States, the Securities and Exchange Commission. A rapidly growing robo-advisor has also caused some controversy over the regulation of such a platform, particularly as it relates to investor protection, fiduciary responsibilities, and fee transparency.

Perhaps the most glaring drawback of robo-advisors is ensuring that the algorithms are not too complicated or hard for a client to understand. In the majority of the platforms which offer customized financial advice, the algorithm becomes so complicated that it will be really hard for the clients to really know how the portfolio is being managed. The lack of transparency might result in a negative impact on the formation of trust if the clients feel that the algorithms are not approaching their best interest almost sufficiently.

Market Volatility and Risk Management: Robo-advisers are pretty much algorithm-based but rely strongly on history for making the investments. However, if extreme volatility becomes the message of the day in the markets, then it becomes most likely that such an algorithm may delay the pertinent actions to temper their risks to some extent. There always may be occasions when the robots need some human-guided interventions to stay in the game during turbulent periods.

Data Privacy and Security: Since the fact remains that robo-advisors collect sensitive personal and financial data in large numbers, it becomes absolutely important to ensure that security over that data is not compromised. Such platforms have to abide by data protection laws such as GDPR in Europe and others that exist around the world.

Taking all these challenges into account, the robo-advisors are becoming increasingly popular and innovative; indeed, with a changing regulatory framework, these platforms probably will remain at the foundation of modern wealth management.

6.5 INVESTMENT PLATFORMS AND CROWDFUNDING

Investment platforms and crowdfunding have transformed the way people invest. They can now invest in different asset classes and industries, which were previously not within the reach of institutional investors or high-net-worth individuals. With equity crowdfunding and real estate crowdfunding, people can access unique investment opportunities while facilitating peer-to-peer investment models. These platforms allow startups, real estate projects, and other ventures to raise capital directly from the public without going through traditional financial institutions and intermediaries. Through technology, investment platforms democratize investment opportunities and enable investors to diversify their portfolios with lower capital commitments.

6.5.1 Equity Crowdfunding: A New Way to Invest

The raising of equity through the process whereby an investor receives some stake in an early-stage company for money invested that may eventually make him or her a shareholder is what is known as equity crowdfunding. This form of investing, in comparison to most investment options, allows investment into private companies, typically on a very early developmental level, thereby carrying the prospect of significant risk and sometimes huge returns. Online, investors can see business plans, forecasts, and even other relevant papers before investing or growing a venture with crowdfunding, getting their nod to begin.

Among the most important attractive features of equity crowdfunding are opportunities for diversification, by which investors own small fractions of several startup ventures or projects. This democratizes the process of investing where average investors' access is opened to opportunities that hitherto were available to only venture capitalists or angel investors. However, while equity crowdfunding opened new avenues for investment, they also are associated with significant risks in terms of potential loss of capital, illiquidity, and lack of control over company decisions.

6.5.2 Real Estate Crowdfunding

Real estate crowdfunding is perhaps the more popular subset of crowdfunding where individual investors combine their money to put towards a real estate project. This allows people to buy real estate without that kind of very high, very traditional upfront cost typically involved with owning property. It brings together investors and developers or real estate companies wanting to raise funds for an apartment building, commercial facility, or mixed use building.

These platforms typically often allow investing in real estate ventures using as low as $500 to $1,000, which can thereby open doors to accessibility in the market that was erstwhile unattainable. Investors may choose either to buy a single property or buy a whole portfolio of properties. Usually, the same platforms give the option to make both equity as well as debt-based investments. With real estate crowdfunding, investors can earn returns through rental income, property appreciation, or interest payments on loans. However, like any investment, real estate crowdfunding carries risks, including market fluctuations, property management issues, and the potential for delayed or non-existent returns.

6.5.3 How Investment Platforms facilitate Peer-to-Peer Investment

Peer-to-peer, or P2P, investment is now possible through investment platforms, which connect individual investors directly with borrowers or projects seeking capital. Through such platforms, investors can finance small businesses, real estate projects, or loans without going through traditional financial institutions such as banks. This model cuts out intermediaries, reduces fees, and offers more favourable terms to both parties.

For instance, in a standard P2P lending model, investors lend money to people or businesses for some interest payments over time. The benefit for the borrowers is the lower interest rate compared to what they could get if they borrowed from banks. Similarly, crowdfunding models can have investors fund start-ups or projects and then share in the success or failure of the ventures that they are investing in. The following tools and features are available for users from investment platforms to track investments, evaluate the risk attached to individual projects, and diversify portfolios across asset classes and geographical regions.

For example, these equity crowdfunding websites provide more routes through which investors can invest in getting equity in private companies. Equally, they form a rather alternative source of venture capital funding for emerging startups. Indeed, P2P lending and crowdfunding have shaped the capital market into something even more fluid and dynamic whereby an individual can lend or invest in a project or business he believes in with the hope of making returns on his investment.

6.5.4 Key Platforms and Their Features: Fundrise, Crowdcube, Seedrs

There are several investment platforms that have come up with features and focus areas unique to each of them. This makes it easier for individual investors as well as project creators to access funding opportunities in various investment models.

Fundrise: Fundrise is one of the leading real estate crowdfunding companies that allows investors to pool funds together to invest in any kind of real estate projects. The company offers a variety of investment options, such as eREITs and eFunds, which expose investors to residential and commercial properties. Fundrise targets investors who are looking to diversify their portfolios with real estate assets and provides a low minimum investment requirement. The platform uses technological mechanisms to manage risk in returns maximization through the computer-automated portfolio. The company offers debts in equity investment options thus creating room for making the real estate accessible to all.

Crowdcube: Crowdcube is a UK-based equity crowdfunding marketplace where startups and developing companies interact with investors seeking share or equity in return for a cash injection. It gives investors an opportunity to invest in early-stage companies with high returns on investment. Crowdcube has campaigns of a wide variety, cutting across different sectors, including technology, food and drink, retail, and healthcare, among others. This allows investors to find projects easily according to their interest. Also, Crowdcube has both primary and secondary market investments thus leaving space for investors who would want to support a new venture or purchase shares in an already existing venture.

Seedrs: Seedrs is another significant equity crowdfunding platform that operates within the UK and Europe. It allows individual investors to invest in early-stage businesses. The platform has various types of startups and growth companies, including technology, media, and renewable energy. It also enables investors to build diversified portfolios across different industries. That allows users to buy and sell interests in shares on a secondary market, thereby adding liquidity to investments that otherwise could not be liquidated. Seedrs also carries out extensive due diligence on businesses it lists to help better inform investors.

All these help democratize the access of investment opportunities in ventures otherwise inaccessible to the smaller investors. They facilitate a much more transparent funding process in which the investment is passed directly to entrepreneurs and companies in ways beneficial to the parties involved.

From conclusion, investment platforms and crow funding have opened new avenues towards investment for both the smaller investors and entrepreneurs through easier access to capital. Of course, this new avenues bring greater accessibility; this is with the price: risks involved, meaning for investors to conduct very deliberate research on each possible and long-term potential for some challenges in an investment option.

6.6 CRYPTOCURRENCY AND BLOCKCHAIN IN INVESTMENT MANAGEMENT

Cryptocurrencies and blockchain technology are heralding tremendous change in investment management; new opportunities and risks emerge from this revolutionary approach to financial transactions. Though in development, these technologies are gaining entry into investment portfolios as well as wealth management practices. They are considered promising more transparency, security, and efficiency at the same time raising significant challenges because of volatility and regulatory uncertainties. This is where knowledge of cryptocurrencies and blockchain comes in; that is, the kind of knowledge required in today's investor seeking to take advantage of the same.

6.6.1 Understanding Cryptocurrencies and Blockchain Technology

Cryptocurrencies are digital currencies using cryptographic techniques for securing transactions and also the control of new units creation. Bitcoins, Ethereum, and other cryptocurrencies operate through decentralized networks referred to as blockchains. Blockchain is the sort of technology in the form of distributed ledgers. They have enabled transactions to be conducted with all aspects- including a guarantee that transactions were created safely, transparently, and are also immobile in a blockchain record. Since it's a decentralized approach, there is no use for any intermediary banking facility. Intermediaries make way for fewer possibilities for fraud and manipulative operations while making these transactions more efficient.

Cryptocurrencies, since they are digital, are not linked to any central bank or government and so investors get attracted towards such alternative investments. Blockchain is the underpinning technology behind the cryptocurrencies but far exceeds that of the digital currencies as it could be used for a lot of areas ranging from finance to healthcare and real estate to many others for data and transactions, which could be transparent, secure, and efficient.

6.6.2 Cryptocurrency and the investment portfolios.

Cryptocurrencies have fast-tracked into becoming a new asset class. They are increasingly sought as part of a diversified portfolio. Most investors regard cryptocurrencies such as Bitcoin and Ethereum as an alternative source of value, or even "digital gold," for protection against inflation and money devaluation in case of a downturn in the economy. On the other hand, decentralization could serve as protection against interference by governments or more traditional financial market fluctuations.

There is also an application case about using cryptocurrency as a speculative investment to an investment portfolio: That is when their returns are really very high from investment and they have the potentials of growing it very fast from its volatilities. There is also very important benefit of diversification since the returns tend often not to correlate very highly with the more traditional asset classes, like stocks, bonds, or real estate holdings. This gives cryptocurrencies a possibility of hedging for the investors against market downturn or systemic risks. However, because of their high volatility, cryptocurrencies are regarded as risky assets and therefore include in investment strategies only if one considers the risk appetite and long-term objectives.

6.6.3 Risk and Volatility of Cryptocurrencies

Among the most significant factors to take into account when integrating cryptocurrencies into investment portfolios is the volatility. The value of cryptocurrencies can go wildly up and down within short periods, mainly driven by market speculation, regulatory news, technological changes, and macroeconomic factors. For example, the price of Bitcoin has experienced huge price fluctuations in the past, making it a very unpredictable asset. Volatility may bring huge profits but also huge losses, which makes it a big risk for investors.

One of the things is that this lack of regulation and anonymity that cryptocurrencies bring along have attracted criminal activities like money laundering and fraud. The vagueness about regulations creates further uncertainty since the value and legitimacy of some cryptocurrencies are susceptible to drastic changes brought about by future legislation or government policymaking. Even though there are those which have, totally proscribed or heavily restricted trading with the cryptocurrency, still for most countries, a big question is how such a currency would be described and regulated.

It allows one to be always well-updated on the related information about international regulations, international trade trends.

6.6.4 Perspectives of Blockchain in Clear wealth Management

While cryptocurrencies themselves pose inherent risk due to their volatility, blockchain technology offers a wide range of opportunities through which wealth management can enhance. Blockchain's decentralized as well as transparent nature affirms that all transactions are carried out securely and can therefore be verified by all other participants in the network. This is especially important within wealth management where trust security and accountability are essential components.

Blockchain can help reduce fraud and improve security by providing an immutable ledger of transactions. This would minimize the risk of falsifying transaction histories or mismanaging assets for wealth managers and investors. It can also provide opportunities for automation through smart contracts—the self-executing contracts where the terms are directly written into code. Smart contracts automatically initiate their execution of transactions without some form of intermediary, with faster settlement processes.

With a blockchain, asset management also gets streamlining because once stored in the network records then, all of this may be secured and highly accessed. This, subsequently has the effect of greatly making data integrity and alleviated administrative burden on any managing wealth firm. This is very handy with complex portfolio management especially holding real estate, commodities and private equity, particularly if more than one needs to view the details of an actual transaction. This company's technology to monitor ownership and assets at precise granularity has unlocked the possibilities for fractional ownership models under which investors will be allowed portions of otherwise illiquid assets.

It basically brings about the revolution in the realm of wealth management by providing secured, transparent, and efficient solutions for wealth management and transaction. While investments in cryptocurrencies carry high risks-high reward, it is quite possible that much more stable, secure, and transparent tools might be used in the management of assets as well as in the processing of transactions.

6.7 PERSONAL FINANCE APPS: TOOLS FOR THE MODERN INVESTOR

Personal finance applications have become extremely important tools that modern investors use to administer their finances effectively and correctly. There are several features that are offered by such apps that help track money spent, build budgets, monitor investments, and in general, improve financial knowledge. Among these apps are the popular ones such as Mint, Personal Capital, and You Need a Budget, or YNAB for short. These tools offer the user something different that helps him or her take control of his or her financial journey and thus form an important part of personal financial management.

Mint is most famously known for its budgeting and expense tracking features. It aggregates data from various bank accounts, credit cards, loans, and investments to give a holistic view of a user's finances. Personal Capital, on the other hand, focuses largely on investment tracking and retirement planning, providing detailed information on asset allocation, net worth, and investment performance. YNAB actually takes a more hands-on approach, helping users map out their budgets based upon income and goals, giving emphasis to creating a pro-active financial mindset. These apps enable users to monitor their spending in real-time, set savings goals, and receive alerts about upcoming bills or overspending.

6.7.1 Budgeting and Expenses Tracking to Make Decent Investment Decisions

Generally, effective budgeting and proper expense tracking are crucially foundational to any good investment strategy. Personal finance applications such as Mint and YNAB make categorization of expenses easier and will track cash flow in advance while setting financial goals for users. With real-time insight into where the money is being spent, he or she will see where reductions can be made on some things to invest in alternative areas. Maybe this creates some pattern on what the discretionary money would spend on, such as going out to eat or for entertainment, freeing more funds to be saved and invested.

This links together the user's budget, along with his or her financial goals, with an investment plan, thus helping that user make informed decisions for investments. Personal finance apps can connect to brokerage accounts so that a user gets a clear view of how investments are doing compared to savings goals. This is an holistic approach, which makes it easy for users to align their day-to-day spending with long-term financial goals, hence making it easier to invest consistently and adjust strategies as needed. These apps make for a more disciplined approach toward investing, which would most likely lead to better financial outcomes over time as the users are kept in line with their spending and saving.

6.7.2 The Integration of Investment Management in Personal Finance Apps

Investment management was, traditionally, a separate tool: either a dedicated brokerage account or financial planning software. This has now changed, with the integration of investment management features within personal finance apps. Most modern personal finance apps allow users to view all their investments in one place, giving them an overview of their overall portfolio. The platform on Personal Capital will deliver good investment tracking capability as well as a much fuller breakdown of asset allocation, returns, and retirement planning projections.

Other personal finance apps are also joining the robo-advisory services that give out automatic investment advice that follows their financial situation and what they want to achieve in life. It is rather helpful to the new beginner investor who may not understand or have the capacity and time to actively manage various portfolios. The apps make it work by asking for a few short questions pertaining to risk tolerance and finances, then automatically giving suggestions on an investment strategy for their needs. This seamless integration of investment management helps make it easier for the users to balance everyday finances with long-term wealth-building strategies, thereby simplifying the complexity often related with managing multiple financial accounts.

6.7.3 Impact on Consumer Behaviour and Financial Literacy

Consumer behaviour and financial literacy have highly increased with personal finance applications. Today, users find themselves immediately accessing financial information, hence becoming more proactive and knowledgeable about their money choices. Such applications very easily allow users to trace how they spend their money, set goals, monitor their investments, and consequently increase financial responsibility. Users are less ignorant of their finances as the application reminds and notifies them continually of their financial health.

Further, the use of financial education in these applications promotes better financial literacy. Most platforms offer articles, tutorials, and tips that will help users understand budgeting, investing, and debt management. This is priceless for those who never had a formal background in financial education. Therefore, there will be the increase of users in the position to make decisions, which will lead them to avoid falling into the debt hole or unwise investment. Personal finance applications will empower consumers to manage their financial futures and hence able to make the correct decision through the de-complication of complex concepts regarding finances and their access.

Such tools help transform the modern investor, bringing along budgeting and tracking expenses, in addition to providing an integrated investment management. It assists in helping to improve consumer behaviour as financial discipline is promoted through giving insights to make well-informed decisions. Adding financial literacy tools, such applications are guiding users into understanding personal finance better; in turn, this gives more responsible, informed, and confident investors.

6.8 ARTIFICIAL INTELLIGENCE AND MACHINE LEARNING IN INVESTMENT

Artificial Intelligence and Machine Learning are transforming the investment management landscape, offering more complex data-driven strategies that enhance decision-making and optimize portfolio performance. Investors can now analyze large volumes of data in real time, which would otherwise be nearly impossible to obtain manually. Through AI and ML algorithms, investment managers are in a position to make better risk assessments, predict movements in the market, and find better ways to optimize allocations to the portfolio. More efficiently and effectively would their investments be.

6.8.1 AI in Investment Strategies: From Risk Assessment to Predictive Analysis

AI has dramatically modified how investment strategies are drawn, especially in terms of risk assessment and predictive analysis. These classic risk management models rely on historical data and statistical techniques. AI does this with much greater extensions by involving significant amounts of real-time data, including news feeds, social media, and market sentiments for the prediction of market trends and risks. For example, usage of Natural Language Processing allows AI systems to analyze financial news and earnings calls, even social media in terms of sentiment analysis so that investors can judge the market sentiment more correctly.

In predictive analysis, AI identifies patterns and trends that are not obvious to human analysts. Machine learning models analyze millions of data points and predict the price of stocks, fluctuations in currency, or even the likelihood of market crashes based on a combination of historical performance and real-time data. This predictive power allows investors to make better decisions, minimizing risks and maximizing returns by acting on insights before others in the market.

6.8.2 Role of Machine Learning in Portfolio Optimization

Machine learning has an important role in the process of portfolio optimization since it's an ever-evolving analysis and adjusting the portfolio to maximize the returns and minimize the risks. Traditional portfolio management methods use static models, while machine learning can be a dynamic approach to portfolio optimization as it considers many aspects, such as asset correlation, market volatility, and global economic conditions. Some reinforcement learning-based machine learning algorithms can make real-time changes to portfolios based on changes in the markets.

Besides, ML algorithms are also able to evaluate and optimize asset allocations based not only on the traditional financial metrics but also on the newer alternative data such as environmental, social, and governance factors that are now critical to investors. Therefore, portfolio managers can align their investment portfolios to a particular person's risk appetite, goals, and preferences as well as adapt to these changing conditions in the marketplace. In this regard, such levels of accuracy and pliability yield a significant comparative advantage pertaining to the optimisation of long-term wealth creation.

6.8.3 Algorithmic Trading: Advantage and Disadvantages

Algorithmic trading is used to describe buying and selling trades automatically and electronically in a computer-programmed procedure based on parameters like volume, price and timing among others. Such algorithms can process vast amounts of data in real time and identify trends at speeds that are unattainable by human capabilities. The first advantage of algorithmic trading is the ability to remove human emotion from the trading decision-making process, which can be costly. Algorithms rely on data-driven models, allowing them to make objective decisions and improve efficiency and consistency in the market.

Algorithmic trading is also associated with risks. One of the biggest concerns is flash crashes or extreme market volatility. Algorithmic trading systems work according to predefined parameters, and therefore, may sometimes exaggerate price movements based on their reaction to changes in the market. In addition, sophisticated algorithms created by various market players are vulnerable to exploitation and can be used to snatch away the markets or offer uneven playing fields to the small investors since they might not have access to the advanced tools. Also, dependency on algorithms creates a deficiency of human monitoring and can create unwanted consequences in case the algorithms are exposed to unexpected market events.

6.8.4 Main AI-Powered Platforms in Wealth Management

In this realm of wealth management, several AI-driven platforms have entered to provide high customization and automate investment services using machine learning and AI technologies. Using robo-advisory services, predictive analytics, and real-time portfolio optimization will deliver the best experience to their clients.

Two of the most popular robo-advisors apply AI and ML algorithms to the optimization of portfolios are Betterment and Wealthfront. They assess clients' risk tolerance, financial goals, and time horizons in order to automatically adjust assets in a diversified portfolio. Both Betterment and Wealthfront offer portfolio optimization by tax-loss harvesting and automatic rebalancing; however, Wealthfront pairs these services with financial planning tools.

Another important AI-driven platform that BlackRock has is Aladdin. This is used in order to provide risk management and portfolio optimization to institutional investors. The system aggregates data from several sources, with machine learning algorithms predicting the market trend and risks on a global scale.

SigFig also provides wealth management that encompasses AI along with human advisors; hence, investors get the best of both worlds. The system mainly depends on AI to understand market trends and automate trades while suggesting necessary adjustments for portfolios in real time. Additionally, access is provided to humans for more complex needs for investment.

Indeed, AI platforms are remodelling the world of wealth management. They offer low-cost, personalized investment solutions previously accessible only to high-net-worth individuals, thereby making investing more accessible and efficient for the masses through automation, AI, and data analytics. Yet, as these technologies mature, regulation, transparency, and how to ensure the AI systems make ethical and unbiased decisions will persist.

6.9 DATA-DRIVEN INVESTMENT INSIGHTS

Big data and advanced analytics transformed wealth management where investors can make much more informed and precise investment decisions. Big data, including vast market trends, economic indicators, consumer behaviour, and alternative data sources, has enabled wealth managers to provide personalized and more effective investment strategies. Big data enables investors not only to analyze past performance but also to predict future market movements that will significantly enhance decision-making processes.

6.9.1 The role of big data in wealth management

Big data is highly important in the modern wealth management system since it gives information that goes beyond financial metrics. Wealth managers and investors can now access large data from various sources, including social media, news articles, transaction data, and even weather patterns, all of which affect market trends. Using this data allows wealth managers to find new market trends, observe changes in real time, and make more accurate predictions on investment opportunities.

Essentially, such analysis can reveal a pattern in terms of the behaviour of consumers, where investors spot these growth sectors ahead of competition. It can also consider large volumes of unstructured data, including sentiment through news feeds or social networks, to know how such markets are going to act in response to a set of events. This fosters a much better perspective of the market, increasing both long-term strategy formulation and short-term decision making.

6.9.2 Use Predictive Analytics for Smart Investment Decisions

Predictive analytics is one of the prime tools of wealth management. It assists investors in making better decisions by predicting future trends based on historical and real-time data. Predictive models can scan vast datasets to identify patterns and correlations that would be impossible to observe otherwise. These models can predict future price movements of stocks, commodities, currencies, and even emerging sectors. They offer an investor an upper hand in the marketplace.

Predictive analytics frequently use machine learning, a category of AI, in an effort to make better predictions. These algorithms refine their models with new data and respond to changes in market conditions. Predictive analytics, therefore, will assist the wealth managers in knowing their best-performing assets, their risk potentials, and how best to optimize portfolios for a better investment choice. By using predictive analytics and combining real-time data, the investors will be able to act quickly on market shifts that may arise and avoid a risk or catch an opportunity before it becomes untimely.

6.9.3 Data-Driven Investment Strategy Personalization

One of the most significant breakthroughs is that an investment strategy can be tailored to match a particular financial objective, risk profile, and needs of the individual or family. Great amounts of data can now be used to identify individual financial profiles and deliver appropriate customized investment solutions. In using big data for personalization, portfolios created from closer alignment to objectives on growth, income generation or capital preservation have been permitted.

AI and machine learning algorithms make personal investment strategies more robust, as they can continually assess and change portfolios according to the ever-changing market conditions and preferences of investors. The outcome is that this type of investment management is not static but rather dynamic because portfolios are constantly optimized. Personalized strategies also allow for stronger client relationships, since the investor feels that his special circumstances are taken into consideration and addressed.

6.9.4 Challenges of Data Security and Privacy

Even though big data promises to bring much promise for improving wealth management, several issues arise with regard to security and privacy when it comes to big data. The amounts of sensitive personal and financial information that a wealth manager and an investment firm deal with are enormous. They become easy victims in such cases for cyber attacks. Such breaches can result in huge financial and reputational loss not only for the affected clients but also for the firms that have handled this information.

Big data and AI have also brought into wealth management issues related to how the information is being collected, stored, and used. As more personal and financial data is shared between the client and the wealth manager, so does the risk of unauthorized access. Encryption of data, anonymization, and secure storage become imperative to maintain client trust and meet regulatory standards.

This is further complicated because of the privacy issues now being amplified by regulations on how personal data is processed in Europe, such as under the General Data Protection Regulation. Wealth management firms can only ensure that they fulfil these regulations while using such big data for investment purposes. Innovation and data safety and privacy are some of the biggest challenges in using data-driven investment management ideas.

6.10 ETHICS AND REGULATION IN WEALTH MANAGEMENT

In addition, with the advancement of wealth management through digital platforms and new technologies, it is at the top of the agenda to deal with ethical concerns and to be in regulatory compliance. Where finance and technology interact with consumer data, several concerns arise, including issues related to privacy, investor protection, and the ethics of an investment strategy. Regulations form the foundation for guiding this industry toward responsible practices in protecting investors and ensuring market integrity.

6.10.1 Regulatory Challenges in Digital Wealth Management

The rapid digital growth of wealth management, supported by AI and robo-advisors among others, has ushered a new series of regulatory challenges. Traditional frameworks were meant for face-to-face communication and manual processing but lag behind the pace and scope of digital changes within the financial services sector. In this regard, ensuring accountability, transparency, and fairness are major issues while setting up standards for the traditional model of wealth management with new digital platforms.

This nature of cross-border makes it complex to regulate. Many of these platforms will cross various jurisdictions to serve multiple jurisdictions with different regulatory requirements. It becomes complex to comply with the difference in law in areas like investor protection, AML, and financial disclosure. Thus, there is a move by the regulatory bodies to harmonize more standards and guidelines over digital wealth management, and it remains work in process and somewhat fragmented around the regions.

6.10.2 Data Privacy Concerns and Consumer Protection

There are increasing data privacy concerns in wealth management using a data-driven investment approach. Personal financial data collected, stored, and analysed poses essential questions regarding to whom such access is accorded and how such access is protected. Wealth management firms should comply with data privacy laws such as the General Data Protection Regulation in Europe or the California Consumer Privacy Act in the United States, which have specific requirements on the processing and sharing of personal data.

Consumer protection is another significant aspect of regulatory issues. As the use of digital wealth management tools increases among more and more individuals, from the underserved or underbanked population, investments should be secure, with no misleading or taking advantages on the part of digital platforms. The regulation framework must ensure that the digital wealth management tools are offering transparent fees, clear risk disclosures, and fair advice to the new investors.

6.10.3 Ethical Investing and ESG Factors

Ethical investing has become quite the hot topic in the past few years, especially due to the term ESG investing, which is in general referred to as taking into consideration Environmental, Social, and Governance factors during an investment decision. Most of the investors today think about making sustainable and socially responsible investments, trying to be aligned with their values at all times. The offering of digital wealth management companies is increasingly including ESG factors, which enables customers to make choices in relation to investing in companies interested in environmental sustainability, best labour practices, and excellent governance.

This shift raises ethical questions on the transparency and the measurability of the performance on ESG factors. For example, one has an increasing concern on "greenwashing," in which companies or funds overstate their efforts toward sustainability in order to attract the socially conscious investor. Regulatory bodies are working to develop clear standards and disclosures to help investors make informed decisions. As ethical investing grows more mainstream, the roles of regulators will be imperative to ensure that these investments are truly sustainable and that their values are aligned with the values of investors.

6.10.4 Future Trends in Regulation and Compliance

As digital wealth management grows, the future trends of regulations and compliance will be towards further development of more powerful technology-driven regulatory frameworks. Therefore, in the wake of innovation, regulators would balance consumer protection and market stability. This is a sector where development of RegTech will go on helping in the implementation of more streamlined compliance obligations by automated mechanisms and real-time monitoring across wealth management firms.

The critical trend will be the standardization of global norms on digital wealth management. There will be greater convergences of rules of investor protection, data privacy, and the use of AI in making financial decisions. This would also lead to more importance being attached to algorithm transparency to make sure that automated decision-making processes remain ethical and answerable, especially as the influence of AI and machine learning grows in investment strategy.

Financial inclusion will be one of the emerging trends. With open access to wealth management, opening it up to the masses, including the poor and the young investor, means there will be over-leveraging, fraud, and misrepresentation. It will have a huge focus on making sure new wealth management platforms are accessible, safe, and fair to all users but put a great focus on consumer education and financial literacy.

The regulatory framework will be shaped by the landscape of digital wealth management as it continues to balance consumer protection with innovation and financial inclusion.

6.11 FUTURE OF INVESTMENTS AND WEALTH MANAGEMENT IN FINTECH

This will be the future of investments and wealth management in the fintech: a cocktail of old methods from decades ago and today's technological innovations. Apparently, a blurred line continues to seem to move ahead along this digital landscape of traditional wealth management and solutions that exist in fintech. More investors would like to see the human expertise and automated systems open doors for a hybrid model that combines the best of both worlds. Combining digital tools with traditional approaches will provide clients with more personalized, efficient, and flexible wealth management options, ultimately redefining the wealth management experience.

6.11.1 Integration of Traditional and Digital Wealth Management

The core of the changes that will continue to drive future industry developments is a seamless confluence of best-of-breed traditional wealth management practices and modern, emerging digital solutions. While old-school wealth management provides great value in its one-to-one, hands-on method, fintechs transformed the way people gain investment services. In the near future, wealth managers will embrace hybrid models that apply digital tools such as robo-advisors, AI, and big data analytics in combination with human financial advisors. This blend will allow firms to present highly customized advice based on comprehensive data analysis while keeping the personal touch that most investors value.

This will enable clients to have a much more fluid interaction with a digital platform managing routine tasks such as portfolio rebalancing and investment monitoring and freeing financial advisors for more complex work in areas of estate planning, tax optimization, and personal risk management. The hybrid model will also be easier to scale and bring sophisticated wealth management to a much wider universe of investors, independent of asset size.

6.11.2 Trends in Artificial Intelligence and Automation

AI and automation have been the leading causes of gigantic transformation in the wealth management sector, and their roles are bound to increase over the years. AI has modified how investment strategies are crafted and administered. With predictive analytics, AI can process and analyze vast amounts of financial data to predict market trends, analyze risks, and make investment decisions with improved accuracy. Automated systems based on changing market conditions allow for continuous learning and improvement in delivering better results with time.

Automation is also making processes in wealth management firms faster, cheaper, and efficient. Automated systems are performing routine functions such as rebalancing, compliance checks, and report generations; thus, the burden shifts to wealth managers in higher-value tasks. More importantly, as AI and automation continue to grow, it will unlock increasingly sophisticated tools for risk management, fraud detection, and customer service, thereby bringing to fore a more agile and responsive wealth management ecosystem.

6.11.3 The Expanding Role of Robo-Advisors and Hybrid Solutions

Robo-advisors, relying on algorithms to provide automated investment guidance and manage portfolios, are likely to play a significantly greater role in the future of wealth management. Costs, simplicity, and higher accessibility will all promote these solutions, which have received strong support from young investors who respond to convenience and low cost. The next evolution will involve sophisticated robo-advisors, using AI-driven insights and advanced risk profiling and real-time market analysis, to present scalable, personalized investment strategies.

A completely digital approach, however, is not likely to fit the bill for many investors, especially those with more complex financial needs. That is why hybrid models, in which robo-advisors work in conjunction with human advisors to deliver holistic wealth management, are gaining traction. In these models, robo-advisors would be used for mundane investment-related activities and human financial advisors would provide advice on such matters as tax planning and retirement objectives. The blend of algorithmic investment with human expertise will provide investors with a more holistic form of wealth management, helping to fill the gap that technology is leaving in favour of customized service.

6.11.4 Future of Cryptocurrency in Portfolios

Cryptocurrencies are increasingly becoming part of investment portfolios and are likely to be on the increase in the future within wealth management. In the view of institutional investors, as they increasingly hold assets such as Bitcoin and Ethereum, cryptocurrencies are coming to be regarded less and less as speculative investments and more as legitimate asset classes. Although volatility and very significant gains remain appealing for investors, so too does a means to diversify as well as hedge against more traditional risks within the market.

Perhaps in the near future these will be the things that actually get to see cryptocurrencies far more widely included within portfolios as wealth managers increasingly recognize the benefit of blockchain technology and safe, transparent investment solutions. With the maturation of regulatory frameworks involving cryptocurrencies, investors would significantly find it easier in treading legal and security implications of investing in a fully digital world. Even as regulatory uncertainty, price volatility, and cybersecurity concerns all remain key hurdles before making it through to being taken seriously as mainstream part and parcel of wealth management's portfolio.

In a long time perspective, cryptocurrencies in investment portfolios would perhaps be defined by their abilities to fit into conventional vehicles and be more clear cut in regulatory terms. A maturing technology, maybe blockchain will usher new channels for highly efficient asset management, transaction across borders and even tokenization of the real world assets into possibly the most potent vehicle that can be applied to strategies in investments.

We see in the future how the wealth management industry will change with all these digital technologies, namely AI, robo-advisors, and even cryptocurrency. Investment strategies will be transformed, and new client experiences will be expected from these innovations inculcated into traditional practices of wealth management.

CHAPTER 7

INSURTECH AND RISK MANAGEMENT

7.1 INTRODUCTION TO INSURTECH

Definition and Overview of Insurtech

The term insurtech refers to the combination of the words "insurance" and "technology." In short, insurtech is the application of innovative technologies to transform and modernize the insurance sector. The purpose of this emerging industry is to build new efficiencies, enhance the customer experience, and transform how insurance products are developed, sold, and managed. Most technologies, including artificial intelligence, machine learning, blockchain, the Internet of Things, and big data analytics, drive innovations in insurtech to challenge traditional models. It is done in a way to come up with more accessible and affordable products while improving their operational efficiency.

From the total insurance platform based on pure paper to application of advanced technological services for use in underwriting procedures, and even in claims handling and customer interaction. Actually, it has gained ground in the past ten years since startup companies as well as established ones realized the technology could come out to produce innovation for this industry of insurance which has a very long history.

7.1.1 Why Insurtech has Kept Moving Forward

There are several key factors, which have led to rapid growth of insurtech in the last couple of years. Consumer pressure to achieve more convenience with increased transparency pushes the insurance industry toward a digital transformation strongly. The growing experience with digital technologies in other sectors naturally makes consumers expect the same levels of accessibility and personalization for their insurance, which is particularly pronounced within newer generations who prefer on-demand, mobile-first user-friendly platforms.

The other major driver for change is the advancement in the technology itself. Advances in AI, big data, and IoT have provided the insurers with tools to offer personalized insurance, improve the assessment of risks, and to streamline operations. AI algorithms and machine learning are also now used to analyze such huge data sets, empowering insurers to make more correct predictions about risks and tailor premiums to individual tastes. Blockchains are also increasing as they enable the promotion of transparency and reduction of fraud with the use of immutable, decentralized records for insurance transactions.

7.1.2 Regulatory Environment

The regulatory environment is also changing with the growing digital insurance solutions and how governments and regulators adapt to the changes. It has been accompanied by increasing competition from non-traditional players, forcing the traditional players to use more technology-driven approaches in a bid to remain relevant in this fast-changing market.

7.2 INSURANCE PLATFORMS

Digital Insurance Platforms: Transformation in the Buying Process Digital Platforms

These modern digital insurance platforms will transform and upgrade the interactions of customers with insurers and finally obtain insurance coverage. High technology digitalized systems present a convenient online and off-line, quicker, faster, and seamless system far from that the traditional offered as majorly paper-oriented and tedious processes. Today, the customer can receive quotes, compare policies, purchase coverage, and even follow up on claims online or through a mobile application by using some digital platforms. This has made it quicker, more transparent, and accessible.

Ease of user interface, instant generation of quotations, and current policy are the most significant features of the digital insurance platform. Most of these systems apply cloud computing, which enables them to store and process large volumes of data with efficiency and security. In that regard, insurers can afford to offer more personalized services to customers, for example, coverage based on behaviour, location, or preference, which is a facilitator of customer satisfaction as well as reducing the cost of policy administration.

7.2.1 Embedded Insurance: Integration of Insurance Products into Other Services or Platforms

Embedded insurance is defined as the direct integration of insurance products into other services or platforms where it becomes easier for the customer to buy coverage in the context of a greater transaction or experience. A good example would be a travel insurance that automatically appears when booking flights or car insurance accompanying the purchase of a car. This removes the friction usually associated with the purchase, then buying an insurance by presenting at point of need and thereby more pertinent and timelier.

This is mostly because the vast majority rise of embedded insurance arises because of the burgeoning ecosystems in which companies increasingly provide chains of interconnected services. This model is, in addition to being convenient for consumers, making it seamless to tap into new customer bases, with the collaboration of non-insurance companies, such as e-commerce platforms, car manufacturers, and even giants in tech. Embedded insurance is, therefore, improving the reach and penetration of insurance products in markets where consumers had never previously considered coverage.

7.2.2 Marketplace Models: Comparison of Peer-to-Peer and Traditional Insurance Models

With insurtech companies taking the lead, it has sent the marketplace models of insurance into a complete reversal. Among these trends thrown out by the revolution are shifting towards P2P or peer-to-peer platforms, which greatly differ from traditional models. In this, the latter pools the risk as they allow the former to collect premiums from the policyholders and accumulate risk. However, P2P allows a group of individuals to distribute the risks amongst them selves, usually by a tool that helps make that happen.

P2P systems typically allow users to establish small groups, or "pools," consisting of like-minded people that have similar risks, be it car insurance or homeowner's insurance. The shared premiums are then paid by the pool to cover those losses within the pool. Any surplus then can be repatriated to the pool members or kept in reserve within the pool for eventual usage. The most fundamental benefit derived from this P2P insurance is probably that of a lower premium with minimal administrative overhead and at low cost, primarily by removing intermediaries.

Although P2P insurance models are on the rise, the traditional model is still leading in the market, particularly in the complex areas such as health and life insurance, in which regulation and financial solvency need to be considered. Yet, with the rise of P2P models and marketplace models, one can see how insurance is heading toward more consumer-centric and community-based models.

7.2.3 Blockchain in Insurance: How Blockchain is Enhancing Transparency and Reducing Fraud

This would therefore give insurance industry Blockchain as the game-changer to enable improvement in transparency and operation efficiency and reduction of fraud. All transactions with this technology are recorded, yet they cannot be modified; hence it is convenient in the insurance sector mostly anchored on trust and security. An insurance company implementing blockchain will be able to create a transparent ledger in claims processing, policyholder records, and transactions to ensure that data is safe, accurate, and available to all parties.

This reduces fraud because the blockchain is structured in such a way that makes it quite difficult to manipulate data or make false claims. In fact, all transactions having a recorded record in an open ledger, insurance firms can easily track claims and ascertain their validity. Secondly, due to self-executing and coded smart contracts on blockchain, claim payment processes will become automated without an intermediary and hence the faster and more accurate claims process; thereby reducing the administrative costs by a very great extent and making customer experience much better.

7.2.4 AI and Machine Learning in Insurance: Personalization of Policies, Underwriting, and Claims Management

Artificial intelligence and machine learning are changing the way insurance companies personalize policies, rate risk, and service claims. AI and ML algorithms can assess big data on everything-from what customers do and are up to medically speaking through what they drive-on top of that, giving custom solutions for insurance services. This has enabled the insurers to have more customized prices for better coverage options rather than lump sums of broad categories like demography.

Underwriting AI models can process data much faster and more accurately than a human underwriter. Therefore, this leads to decisions being made in real time based on many factors. This leads therefore to more accurate risk assessments and better pricing and fewer claims denials. In addition, AI plays a significant role in claims management, where machine learning algorithms can detect fraud, predict claims outcomes, and automate claims processing, leading to faster settlements.

Moreover, AI-based chatbots are used in the process of handling customer queries and policy management, and it will also be applied for the processing of claims which would result in efficiency as well as better customer experience. As AI and ML develop, insurance will find even more of these applications in improving operational efficiency while saving costs and delivering more for consumers.

7.3 AUTOMATION OF CLAIMS PROCESSING

Automated Claims Handling: Use of AI, Chatbots, and RPA in Claims Processing

Automated claims handling has transformed the insurance industry through the ease of making entire submissions, evaluation, and settlement of claims. Insurers can now handle massive volumes of claims much more rapidly with greater accuracy as a result of applying AI, chatbots, and RPA in claims processing. Claims will be instantly evaluated by AI-based systems based on the inputs made; there will also be 24/7 chatbot support for filling up claims, answering queries, or even guiding customers in the process.

RPA can reduce the human interdependence in doing repetitive functions such as data entry, verification of policies, and document handling, thus accelerating the settling of claims. This ensures lesser mistakes on the side of humans, and there is overall greater efficiency within the process. It enhances customer experience, too, where quicker settlement of claims can be given, in operational efficiency improved, and the administrative cost in the processing of claims is cut by automation.

7.3.1 Claims Fraud Detection: Using AI and Machine Learning to Detect Frauds in Claims

Fraudulent claims are very important issues in the insurance business and result in large monetary losses. The battle against fraud has become immensely crucial with AI and machine learning (ML), because processing huge data for a possible pattern or deviation would show fraudulent activity. One may try applying those algorithms to the old data to get more precision accuracy; even the fraud indicator in a piece of incongruous information could emanate from overstated claims, which might completely lie outside the normal behaviour of claims.

Even the most suspicious claims can be alerted before they get a payment using the support of advanced analytics, and then it only has lesser chances of fraud while the proper flow of genuine claims occurs. Advanced AI-based fraud detection crosschecks claim with outside databases and past claims against which more effective identification can be made than in any traditional way. It provides the insurer an opportunity to take proactive steps in fraud prevention early on and save time and resources with the confidence and integrity of the claim process still intact.

7.3.2 Full-Frontal Automation: Claims Settlement - From Start to Finish

Claims processing end-to-end automation means that from making a claim to finally settling the same, it is made fully automated. Such an approach enhances the speed, efficiency, and accuracy of claims handling. As the process for filing a claim begins, AI automatically fetches and analyses all necessary information, such as details of the policy and proofs through photographs or videos taken at the time of damages. This then means that the RPA tools can authenticate the details of the claim and work on the documentation by allowing the claim to flow into the right approval channels-all without human intervention.

It further contributes to the reduction of delay, such as waiting for human review or even inputting data. Moreover, the consistencies of claims decisions are enhanced because the automated system operates based on pre-set rules and regulations that are not biased to human oversight or biasness. The cutting down on time taken in processing of claims helps in making the entire experience smooth and customer-centric for insurers thus boosting satisfaction and loyalty amongst the customers and their retention.

7.3.3 Blockchain for Claim Transparency: How Blockchain Ensures Claims Management to be Decentralized, Unalterable and Transparent

It is using the power of blockchain technology to make claims processing very transparent and secure. Blockchain creates an immutable, decentralized ledger wherein claims-related data is secured and cannot be altered after entering the same. In such a scenario, each party in the claim process - the claimant and the insurer - can keep a real-time track and verification of the status of the claim.

Blockchain also eliminates fraud by providing an auditable public log of every transaction, which also decreases the chance of altering claims or multiple dipping. Smart contracts are self-executing contracts coded into a blockchain and can automatically accept claims and payments according to predetermined criteria. This will further accelerate settlements, decrease disputes, and ensure claims are made in accordance with the terms that exist in the policy. With higher adoption, its transparency and greater security for claims processing will undoubtedly become the heart of the modern systems in insurance.

7.3.4 Efficiency in Claims Process: It will reduce time and costs and also reduce the manual effort required for making claims.

Improvement in customer satisfaction with low operational costs to the insurers: Efficiency in claims processing is a very effective factor. The process involves automation of several steps. This cuts down settlement times drastically and minimizes the amount of manual effort that is necessary, thus bringing down the administrative costs. For example, AI-powered systems will assess claims instantly, leaving less time for human adjusters to physically inspect damages or review claims.

The paper and phone calls in the manual process eliminate duplication and delays. Online filing of claims, automatic processing of documents, and speeding up of payment approvals can be possible through smart contracts or automated workflows. Predictive analytics can be used for efficient resource allocation to process claims in a cost-effective manner. These outcomes give the lowest possible cost of operations, speedy turnaround time, and satisfaction among the customers. This is how the insurance companies benefit in the achievement of a competitive and profitable business model.

7.4 RISK MANAGEMENT TOOLS

Predictive Analytics: How Predictive Models Help Insurers Assess and Mitigate Risks

Predictive analytics has become the anchor of the insurance industry because it helps insurers evaluate and mitigate risks before these actually happen. Predictive models can accurately determine future occurrences, including even potential claims or loss events, through the application of advanced algorithms and historical data. They study patterns relating to customer behaviour, historical claims, and external elements such as market trends and environmental data for an insurance company to predict possible risk and proactively adjust prices, policies, or coverages.

The main advantage of predictive analytics is that it allows insurers to make decisions based on data and, therefore, reduces uncertainty and increases the accuracy of risk assessments. For example, predictive models can identify high-risk customers early on, thus allowing insurers to offer customized policies or preventive measures that would minimize the chances of future claims. This approach also enables dynamic pricing models wherein the premiums are adjusted as per the expected risk level of an individual or business. This adjustment will improve the competitiveness and profitability of the organization in the market.

7.4.1 Risk Profiling and Underwriting: Big Data, AI, and IoT in their march toward superior risk assessments

Big data, coupled with artificial intelligence and Internet of Things (IoT) has altered so much as far as risk profiling and underwriting is concerned. Where, previously they profiled and even underwrote based on information not even worth using-which includes the age, the gender and medical history. With big data coming all the way from sources from all corners of the globe, though, those insurers can depend on many more detailed, not to mention exact, pieces of information in assessing their risks.

AI and machine learning algorithms go through large datasets, which would include social media activity, purchasing behaviour, even real-time health data, just to better determine a level of risk with an increasingly higher degree of accuracy. IoT devices such as smart home sensors and connected car technology allow for monitoring behaviour in real-time, updating the risk profiles of such an individual. He only pays for a premium based on how fast he goes, when he is braking, and where he's going. That's much more fact than assumptions.

7.4.2 The more detailed the profiling of risks, the more specific premiums are and even more effective risk management will be. Internet of Things (IoT) for Risk Prevention:

IoT Devices such as Smart Home Sensors and Vehicle Telematics for Real-Time Risk Monitoring

IoT has transformed the approach to the prevention of risks in the insurance sector. It provides real-time monitoring of risks through connected appliances. All intelligent smoke detectors, leak sensors, and security cameras offer home insurers real-time data that would otherwise have created huge claims. The leak sensor, for instance, may alert the owner of such impending flooding or water damages so that such events may happen within a couple of moments before it leads to damages so that a good act could be undertaken on their behalf to lessen the consequence of the claim.

IoT-enabled telematics in the auto insurance industry that track drivers' behaviour in terms of speed, acceleration, and braking patterns can provide an insurer with risk levels on the basis of actual behaviour. This means that offering policies based on data points available in real-time gives the insurers incentives to offer discounts for good behaviour while incentivizing safe driving. IoT devices have a very important role to play in monitoring operational risks for businesses. This allows insurers to monitor potential hazards and advise businesses on mitigation strategies in real time.

7.4.3 Cybersecurity risk management: Managing the growing threat of cyber threats in the digital insurance ecosystem.

As insurance companies increase their digital platforms for managing clients' data, cyber threats automatically become an important issue in the risk management strategies. Cyber risk management tools guard sensitive data, including private and financial information, from breaches and cyberattacks. Insurers must implement more robust security measures that assure data integrity, privacy, and regulatory compliance with standards like GDPR and CCPA.

In the wake of increased threats by cybercrimes, some insurers begin to provide cybersecurity risk management as add-ons in their products. In addition to that, cyber insurance specialized policies are offered. That is not all; other types of policies protect businesses against potential financial loss as a result of data breaches, ransomware attacks, and so many more types of cybersecurity breach. The firms utilize high-end security solutions, including encryption, multi-factor authentication, and AI-based threat detection, to safeguard the insurance firms and their customers from cyber risks. These solutions reduce the level of potential damage. Monitoring systems that provide real-time monitoring are utilized by the firms to detect cyber threats quickly and problems and solve them. This gives the reinsurance firm added strength in handling risks.

7.4.4 Reinsurance Technologies: How Technology is Enhancing Reinsurance Processes, Including Risk Pooling and Pricing Optimization

Reinsurance is the process where an insurer buys cover from another insurer to control exposure to risk. Technology has improved reinsurance hugely through the use of highly sophisticated tools in risk modeling and data analytics that enhance pricing, risk exposure evaluation, and pooling of risks. With technology, reinsurers can analyze a much more expansive scope of data such as historical loss data, climate data, and geopolitical factors and therefore make better estimations of claims. Thus, the reinsurers may change their pricing structures with respect to the projection of claims.

Advanced software solutions and AI-based tools also help reinsurance companies automate the underwriting process, which is much more efficient and accurate. Reinsurance companies have access to real-time data and can make dynamic changes to risk pools to ensure that they are sufficiently covered but not overexposed. Blockchain technology may also make reinsurance transactions much more streamlined by making all interactions transparent and immutable, thus reducing the involvement of intermediaries and associated administrative costs.

7.4.5 Risk modeling and simulation: utilize more sophisticated algorithms and better analytics for predictive modeling about the risk in question

Risk modeling and simulation are the backbone of the insurance business today, which has been allowing insurers to better predict and hedge risks with sophisticated algorithms and data analytics. With the help of this feature, insurers can design extensive simulations of all risk events and assess the implications of such changes as the impact of economic factors, a natural disaster, or alterations in customer behaviour on their portfolios.

Advanced risk modeling techniques that include the Monte Carlo simulations and even scenario analysis would enable them to run tens of thousands of simulations in light of an incredibly broad range of possible outcomes. This allows the insurer to understand impacts of various risks on their financials and prepare their strategies well before exposure is made to them. It also enables them to include finer details, such as microeconomic indicators or local weather patterns, to further refine their models. The more these technologies advance, the more insurers will understand and manage risk, hence better equipping them to make data-driven decisions and serve both their customers and bottom lines.

7.5 REGULATORY AND COMPLIANCE CHALLENGES IN INSURTECH

Insuring the Way Through Regulation in the Age of Insurtech

It becomes hard to navigate the regulatory landscapes as insurtech continues to disrupt the traditional insurance. The industry of insurance brings new challenges to regulators because they must adjust their current regulations in line with newer innovations, including digital platforms, blockchain, and artificial intelligence. Traditional laws defining traditional insurance may not be able to keep pace with the cross-border nature of digital platforms, non-traditional data sources, and risks which may emerge from new models of insurtech. In most cases, regulation frameworks regarding the handling of insurtech in operations of a company come under focus, including consumer protection, financial solvency, and transparency in carrying out business activities.

Other regulations might be applied to the digital platforms, cloud computing, and data management. This is one of the main reasons why it is really hard for insurtech businesses to scale a business over borders without really dealing with different compliance requirements. Regulation uncertainty that involves the development of insurtech presents one of the major difficulties that start-ups and other established insurers will have to deal with. Data privacy and security issues

7.5.1 Data privacy and security

It is of utmost concern for any firm dealing with the insurtech business since it gathers, analyses, and holds significant amounts of sensitive data from its customers.

Be it AI-driven underwriting, big data analytics for personalized policies, or digital platforms for claims handling, the insurtech companies have to ensure they are in conformity with the current data protection laws and guidelines, be it GDPR in Europe or CCPA in California in the US. Data breach can lead to data loss, erosion of customer confidence, and prosecution.

The integration of innovative, complex technologies, such as IoT devices, blockchain, or AI, particularly poses great problems with respect to management and the creation of related complex data. Connected health and car insurance devices and others providing constant flows of personal information, which ought to be processed and secured in the most appropriate form, is an excellent example. Most importantly, these must be able to fend off cyber attacks. The insurtech firms should, therefore, develop robust cybersecurity, encryption policies, and open data practices that do not compromise on regulatory compliance but minimize the threat.

7.5.2 The Role Of Regulators In Shaping The Future of Insurtech Regulators

It will play a basic role in ensuring the insurance sector is stable, fair, and secure while the insurtech landscape evolves.

Their objective is to ensure that innovation promotion and consumer protection are both balanced in such a way that the new technologies neither compromise the integrity of the market nor introduce new risks. The regulators are also now part of the conversation, as how the current laws have to be amended to adapt to this increasingly prominent role of technology in insurance and solve the issues posed by the emerging insurtech solutions. The most notable example is "regulatory sandboxes." Those are through which, for example, insurtech companies get to test their products in a controlled setting under the supervision of regulators.

This creates space for innovation and ensures that the regulatory issues are addressed on the other side. The regulators have been exploring frameworks on data governance, cybersecurity, and cross-border insurance operations. As the insurtech space matures, it will be expected that regulators continue to play a crucial role in guiding the sector toward sustainable, fair, and secure practices, but all this while encouraging innovation and competition.

7.6 THE FUTURE OF INSURTECH AND RISK MANAGEMENT

Emerging Technologies and Their Potential Impact

In the near future, quantum computing and AR, among many other advances, are going to significantly alter the landscape of the insurance industry.

For example, it might be theoretically possible for quantum computing to revolutionize how insurers model risk and data analysis. Quantum computers will process tremendous amounts of complex data at speeds never before achieved, which may ultimately let insurers ascertain risks much better and predict claims and therefore better optimize pricing strategies-which in turn would probably lead to more accurate underwriting models and improve industry efficiency as a whole. In an entirely different way, however, the face of interaction between an insurance company and its customer and how risk is being assessed can be modified using augmented reality.

One can virtually conduct a property inspection through AR. Therefore, this means that, to the insurer, data and visuals shall be relayed in real-time with no need for a site visit. For instance, in health insurance, AR can be applied to the personal wellness programs of overlaying real-time health data and predictive analytics onto the user's environment. This will likely contribute more towards the enhanced risk management aspect as it provides several ways of real-time monitoring and mitigation of risks to benefit insurers and policyholders equally. Connecting Insurtech with Other Fintech Innovations

The future of insurtech is not separable from other fintech innovations that form an increasingly connected ecosystem.

Blockchain, artificial intelligence, and big data analytics have already changed the face of an insurance companies' operations, and their integration with other financial services could significantly speed up transformation in the sector. For example, the decentralized nature and security features of blockchain technology could apply not only in claims management and fraud prevention but also make cross sector transactions better and more efficient, including aspects of payment, lending, and insurance product buildout and offers. Finally, AI personal finance tools and insurance platforms could become more integrated within the full-service financial products. Through predictive analytics and recommendation systems, investment advice, insurance policies, and credit management can all be integrated into a single digital space. The disruption and enhancement opportunities of this integration with the more overarching fintech trends hold tremendous potential, offering smarter and more integrated financial solutions for consumers and businesses alike in the reshaping of risk management in insurtech.

Customer-centric models are now slowly but surely changing the dynamics of risk management in the insurtech world.

With standardised coverage, historically, insurance policies fell under broad categories. Today consumers are demanding more and more individualized coverage options that resonate with their specific and behavioural needs. This rising number of digital platforms, combined with an improvement in data analytics, has made it a necessity for insurers to incorporate much more detailed information about their customers, including driving habits, health metrics, and lifestyle choices, so that they can offer products better suited to reflect the true risks of specific customers. This customer-centric approach in risk management implies that the dynamic pricing models can offer when the premium moves with real-time data and changing circumstances.

For instance, pay-as-you-go car insurance can charge people based on actual mileage; health insurers can give rebates to individuals who always engage in wellness activities. The focus of insurtech companies on individual risk profiles not only makes their offerings more specific but also deepens customer relationships by emphasizing mutual trust and personalized service. Co-operation between Traditional Insurers and Insurtech Startups

Although termed a company disrupting the trajectory of the insurance industry, future years will have been ones where a norm of greater mutual cooperation between traditional insurance companies and innovative young firms will have been established. Established companies have industry knowledge, a customer base, and an idea of what is possible in terms of regulatory support, whereas startups bring new approaches with the latest cutting-edge technology and the speed to move fast. Then by collaborating together, both parties can then combine their strength to innovate and enhance the customer experience.

Already, most traditional insurers collaborate with the insurtechs that combine the existing operations with new technologies.

Adoption could take the form of AI usage in claims processing, blockchain for transparency, and IoT devices for risk calculation. The new model accelerates new technology adoption and gives levers to insurance companies that mitigate the inherent risks of technological disruption. More common hybrids that will emerge with this hybrid model, combining the stability and reach of traditional insurers with the innovation and speed of insurtech startups, will make for a more dynamic and robust insurance ecosystem. 7. Case Studies and Industry Examples Successful Insurtech Platforms and Their Impact on the Industry

A number of insurtech companies have entered and changed the face of the insurance industry by killing the old models and presenting innovation at the table. Two examples are Lemonade and Root Insurance.

Lemonade: Lemonade is an AI-driven insurance platform that has dramatically changed the way customers go about buying renters' and homeowners' insurance.

Lemonade is bringing a fully digital and customer-centric experience using artificial intelligence and machine learning; experience through which customers can derive a quote, buy their policies, and file a claim completely online. Along with this, the firm also uses AI chatbots like "Maya" in customer care. That kind of chatbot directly provides support to the holder of the policy. It has also employed a fixed fee model to create a business model where conflict of interest between the insurer and policyholder can be minimized. Lemonade takes the unclaimed premiums for charity, which has transparency and social good to offer and differentiates from other traditional insurers. Many other startups went all in adopting the business model after being witnessed so aggressively, a wave of digital transformation spread throughout the insurance domain. Using AI to make things custom tailored when it comes to coverage, or processing claims will ultimately automate claim processing with more efficiency and transparency customer-centric within an industry.

Root Insurance: Root is insurtech's exemplification of a full-on disruption of the automobile insurance paradigm.

Root uses smartphone technology to analyze driving behaviour, and provides auto insurance based on how safe a certain person drives. The corporation uses telematics plus analysis of data to follow live driving habits in regard to speed, braking and cornering in developing even more accurate and much more individualized pricing model. It actually helps to get rid of all the traditional risk-based pricing mechanisms, which are normally dependent on general demographic data, and offers customized policies for every driver's behaviour. Data analytics and AI usage have helped the company have more competitive pricing and improvement in the risk assessment and even a more transparent, customer-centric experience. It streamlined its journey of customers and cut its operating cost by throwing down the business model for the car insurance business since it removed agents' involvement by using an entirely digital process.

Real-life Applications of Claims Automation and Risk Management solutions in leading Insurance Organizations

Some leading insurance companies are embracing claims automation and risk management solutions as a way of efficiently upgrading performance, saving costs, and ensuring enhanced customer satisfaction. The adoption of said tools in the traditional claim handling process transforms the nature of claims processing, largely with artificial intelligence, big data, and machine learning.

Claims Automation: In this regard, Allianz has only recently embraced an AI-based claims automation system for its claims management process.

The Allianz AI system analyses claims data automatically and recognizes fraudulent claims, hence directly routing the legitimate claims to the appropriate adjusters. This will make the processing of claims faster, minimize administrative costs, and ensure that claims are handled justly and accurately. The Allianz's platform can also process different kinds of claims such as accidents involving autos and property damages by extracting and interpreting data from images and documents. Risk Management Tools: In addition, AXA uses sophisticated risk management tools to better evaluate and mitigate the risks of premium-paying customers. For instance, the company employs the latest AI and big data analytics in real-time to assess risks, especially in natural disaster prediction, vehicle telematics, and health data monitoring. Even its AXA Drive app leans on telematics, where it monitors driver behaviour with recommendations on how people may lower car accidents. And in health insurance, it utilizes wearables that could monitor the fitness and health data of the policyholder so that the risk will be proactively managed as healthy lifestyles are developed with lower premiums. Commercial insurance companies like Chubb have implemented an advanced risk management platform into the systems to evaluate their client's risk profile.

And, in return, Chubb uses data analytics for predicting potential exposures-where the equipment fails, cyber security breach, etc while guiding clients into reducing that kind of risks at that moment when they're not actual claims. This has been a step in that direction, which empowered insurance companies to come up proactively in client's day-to-day activity by extending the scope from the general coverage. These innovations in claims automation and risk management are improving not only the operational efficiency of insurers but also the customer experience with faster claim settlement times, personalized risk mitigation, and overall transparency in the claims process. The general trend is going to continue to transform the insurance industry further with digital transformation and efficiency.

CHAPTER 8

REGULATORY AND COMPLIANCE FRAMEWORKS

8.1 OVERVIEW OF REGULATORY AND COMPLIANCE FRAMEWORKS IN FINTECH

Introduction to Regulatory Challenges in Fintech

As a sector that finds at its very core the interface of finance and technology, Fintech always calls for unique regulatory challenges, where the rapid innovation velocity outpaces regulators' response time for new products and services and business models to come into being. As fintech companies innovate within payments, lending, investment, and insurance, a challenge faces regulators; such an innovation should comply with already existing financial laws but at the same time promote innovation. Here lie the contradictions: between providing consumer protection, maintaining financial sector stability, and fuelling innovation-whose imperatives all revolve round agile, dynamic regulations in a position to update itself as a new fintech landscape emerges.

In addition, fintech companies often operate in a global ecosystem. Many firms provide cross-border services. That means a layer of complexity- firms have to navigate patchworks of regulations across multiple jurisdictions, which differ both in terms of the severity of their stringency and focus and in how their enforcement is implemented. Adapting to such fast-changing technologies as blockchain, AI, and open banking while remaining compliant might be a daunting task in such a dynamic environment.

8.1.1 Importance of Compliance in the Financial Industry

Compliance constitutes an important cornerstone in the financial industry and forms the basis for maintaining integrity as well as stability in the financial markets and protection against fraud, manipulation, or other risks. In respect of fintech, the character of the financial data it manages and the potential threats of digital financial services render compliance even more important. It leads to loss in consumer trust as well as financial fines or the possible legal ramifications if it does not observe regulatory compliance.

In fintech, compliance is extended to many areas. These include anti-money laundering (AML), combating the financing of terrorism (CFT), data privacy, cybersecurity, consumer protection, and financial reporting. Not only do these standards keep the consumers safe but also help the whole financial ecosystem be in a proper working state. Compliance frameworks for such firms will allow them to establish their commitment to doing business securely, ethically, and responsibly. That is basically important in gaining credibility and customers.

8.1.2 Global Key Regulatory Bodies and their Roles

There are lots of global regulatory bodies who have played a very big role in regulating fintech operations and compliance across the borders. Some of these key regulators include:

U.S. Securities and Exchange Commission (SEC): This is one of the primary regulators of securities markets and investor protection in the United States. The commission enforces laws involving trading in securities, public disclosure, and manipulation of markets that affect fintech companies engaged in investment platforms, cryptocurrencies, and crowdfunding.

Financial Conduct Authority (FCA): FCA regulates financial markets in the U.K. and makes sure that financial services firms operate in a fair, transparent, and consumer-friendly manner. It is very active in overseeing fintech developments, especially in areas such as payments, digital banking, and consumer credit.

European Banking Authority (EBA): EBA is the supervisory authority of the banking sector of the European Union, covering fintech services such as payment institutions, e-money, and cryptocurrencies. It offers technical standards and regulatory guidelines for maintaining financial stability and protecting consumers in the EU.

Commodity Futures Trading Commission (CFTC): The CFTC oversees the derivatives markets. This is applicable for those fintech firms working within the cryptocurrency arena or engaged in commodity trading.

Regional Regulations (for example, GDPR in Europe and the Dodd-Frank Act in the U.S.)

General Data Protection Regulation (GDPR) – Europe: This is one of the world's most comprehensive data privacy laws. It comes with quite a significant consequence on the fintechs' activities if they handle or process personal data. GDPR will majorly look at issues such as consumer rights and the transparency regarding personal data use. This standard is applied not only by EU companies but also to all companies processing the data of citizens in the European Union, so it makes sense as a global fintech standard.

Dodd-Frank Wall Street Reform and Consumer Protection Act – U.S.: Dodd-Frank was enacted in 2008 as a reaction to the financial crisis that had just hit the country. It is an act that will increase the transparency of the financial system and, therefore, reduce systemic risk. The act gives directives on regulating consumer financial products, the establishment of the Consumer Financial Protection Bureau, and heavy-duty regulation of derivatives trading. Dodd-Frank includes a wide range of compliance obligations for fintech companies, especially the ones relating to lending, investment, and consumer financial products.

Such regional rules are important to protect the consumer, prevent unfair competition, and make financial markets stable. At the same time, such regional rules pose challenges to fintech companies, especially if their business is cross-border, meaning that they have to comply with multiple and sometimes conflicting regimes of regulation. As fintech increases, the regime of regulation has to change in such a way that these new innovations do not rock the safe, equitable, and transparent financial sector.

8.2 FINANCIAL RULES AND COMPLIANCE

AML and KYC requirements include an important part of financial policies that are engaged to avoid illegal activities of money laundering and financing by the terrorists. AML, short for anti-money laundering, basically describes regulations that are related to monitoring suspected activities of a financial institution on behalf of illegal means or movements of funds through some transactions. The banks, based on KYC regulations, should be in a position to confirm and identify the clients with a view of ascertaining their engagement in legal or illicit activity. This, therefore, helps in playing an essential role towards the preservation of the financial system regarding issues, at the moment, particularly regarding the fintech and the digital payments without borders, and also without anonymity. Fintech companies should have a better set of KYC and AML practices about customer's identity verification, transactional monitoring, and reporting to the concerned authority in cases of suspicious transactions. Therefore, banks always need to be aware of changing rules of compliance which prevent being at risk in terms of legality and reputation.

8.2.1 Payment Services Directive 2, Open Banking

Payment Services Directive 2 is a landmark regulation in the context of the European Union. This enhances payment services across Europe and increases consumer protection. PSD2 obliges banks and payment service providers to open their payment services and customer account information to third-party providers. It thus promotes competition and innovation. This is part of the larger initiative known as Open Banking, which enables fintech companies to access financial data (with customer consent) and offer innovative payment solutions, personalized financial services, and seamless customer experiences.

PSD2, as part of enhancing the transparency and security in the financial sector, includes a more robust authentication and further access to payment services. Third-party providers, therefore, are enabled to provide value-added services like initiation of payments or account aggregation, leading to new financial products and services. This includes budgeting tools, instant payment systems, peer-to-peer lending platforms, among others. But even as PSD2 drives innovation, it also has on its back the fears associated with data privacy and the security of customer information in which financial institutions need to invest to protect against those threats.

8.2.2 The Financial Action Task Force (FATF)

The Financial Action Task Force, commonly referred to as FATF, is a global body formed with objectives of setting policies that could help curb money laundering and terrorist financing among other dangerous threats to the financial structure of the world. During 1989, the organization became objective setting after its role of developing standard global standards for regulating and further boosting support for help towards assisting governments and the financial institutions in the effort to combat illicit financial activity. Countries implement FATF's recommendations worldwide, from which national and regional AML and CFT-based laws are enacted. Thus, the ongoing growth in fintech business in worldwide finance has necessitated growing FATF emphasis on dangers presented by newly emerging technologies, including those of cryptocurrency, digital wallet, or peer-to-peer lending companies. The FATF is now able to ensure that there is no facilitation of illegal activities through innovation in financial services and that, therefore, financial systems should be safe and secure through these emerging sectors guidelines.

8.2.3 Basel III and Capital Requirements

Basel III is a global standard by the Basel Committee on Banking Supervision that establishes requirements for banks to further strengthen regulation, supervision and risk management.

Basel III will give the world's banks tighter capital requirements, liquidity standards, and leverage ratios so that they can better withstand financial shocks and not face future crises. An important component of Basel III is that banks must hold higher levels of common equity tier 1, or CET1, capital. This is the cushion a bank uses in times of financial stress. It further provides with liquidity provisions, such as the liquidity coverage ratio that covers banks short-term liabilities by requiring these banks to have liquid resources that could be used when covering present obligations and finally the net stable funding ratio, obliging banks to fund themselves with more stable sources.

Specifically speaking, this applies to the fintech companies that are engaged in banking or lending because such is the minimum requirement on capital adequacy and risk management. The more integrative fintech becomes part of the traditional banking system, the more banks and fintech firms comply with such capital requirements so that the financial ecosystem can become stable.

8.2.4 Securities Regulations and Enforcement

The Securities regulations are designed to protect investors and promote fair and efficient markets. They also help avoid market manipulation and fraud. Such regulations are enacted by the regulatory bodies of securities, such as the U.S. Securities and Exchange Commission (SEC), the UK's Financial Conduct Authority (FCA), and similar entities around the globe. Securities regulations encompass issues, trading, and reporting of securities, which may include stocks, bonds, and other investment products.

To a fintech firm focused on investment services, which may comprise robo-advisors, crowdfunding sites, and online brokerage houses, securities laws are essential for maintaining standards to ensure compliance with laws on investor protection.

This is comprised of other companies that issue tokenized securities or give out initial coin offerings. Within the cryptocurrency sphere, this category may present challenging tasks in enforcing securities law since such assets can only be possessed digitally. On the other hand, securities regulators are increasingly getting more attention from fintech companies to ensure they provide transparent, fair, and compliant services to investors. The regulators keep themselves in tune with these new market practices, risks, and technologies of financial services by continuously refining the securities laws and their application. Such things include algorithmic trading or blockchain-based securities.

8.3 FINTECH NEW REGULATIONS

Regulation in Cryptocurrency and Blockchain- Europe example: MiCA Regulation and SEC's Approach in the U.S.

The finance world is changing rapidly through blockchain and cryptocurrencies. This has led to regulators who are working on all those new risks and opportunities posed by these new technologies with effective frameworks. Notably, the most effective legislative efforts to regulate European cryptocurrency markets are through a regulation called **Markets in Crypto-Assets Regulation (MiCA).** It aims to create a comprehensive regulatory environment for crypto-asset issuers and service providers. The provisions help ensure investor protection, market integrity, and financial stability. The provisions cover requirements on transparency, disclosure, and anti-money laundering measures, among others.

In the U.S., the **Securities and Exchange Commission** is very cautious but effective in regulating the issuance of cryptocurrencies. Generally, it classifies these as securities, which fall under federal securities laws. This was supposed to be oversight by the SEC aimed at regulating market manipulation and fraud in cryptocurrency trading platforms and also promoting more openness in digital asset markets. It is open to debate whether the SEC adopts a regulation-friendly stance, thereby negatively impacting innovation in space. These regulatory frameworks are pivotal for the sustainable growth of fintech businesses since they establish legal clarity while addressing volatility-related, fraud, and ill activities concerns within the ecosystem of digital assets.

8.3.1 Digital Asset Regulations and Impact on Fintech Companies

At the heart of innovation in fintech is the presence of digital assets: cryptocurrencies, tokenized assets, and stablecoins. The laws governing digital assets are as well evolving rapidly, but each country has developed an own framework on how its digital assets should be administered and traded. There has to be a difference about the way jurisdictions approach regulating and, thus, that becomes a headache for fintech firms when trying to reach other borders. Some places fully integrate digital assets into the financial system, while others are put under restrictions or are forbidden.

Fintech companies dealing in digital assets have to traverse very complex legal landscapes which usually involve regulatory oversight of several authorities, including but not limited to securities regulators, central banks, and financial watchdogs. An example would be that of a fintech company whose tokenized asset must conform to the relevant securities law, which may be highly elaborate reporting and compliance requirements. Furthermore, issues raised would regard the treatment of stable coins, that stable coins linked to fiat currencies, whereas in the United States there is a concern that potential risks of stablecoins upon the financial system could put at risk and the EU regulators are developing frameworks intended to ensure issuers comply with reserve requirements for a stablecoin. Fintech firms must hence remain agile as regulatory clarity continues to evolve, implementing strong compliance measures that mitigate the risks associated with regulation of digital assets.

8.3.2 Data privacy and cybersecurity regulations, for example, CCPA, and GDPR.

Data privacy and cybersecurity are the highest concerns for fintech firms since they operate massively in personal and financial information. Among the most key regulations influencing the data of the fintech companies is the **General Data Protection Regulation** from Europe and the **California Consumer Privacy Act** from the United States. The GDPR of 2018 is actually the new standard for protecting data globally. It outlines requirements where companies must have proper defences for personal data and respect transparency in collecting such practices as well as an ability to exercise control with information. The regulation prescribes grave fines for violations, giving fintech companies ample incentives to implement suitable data-protection measures.

Similarly, the CCPA gives California residents rights over their personal data, rights to know what is being collected, rights to delete data, and rights to opt out of data sales. It is the same as in GDPR, making a company take proactive measures on securing customer data and keeping fintech firms alert and vigilant on their cybersecurity measures in the protection of sensitive financial information. As cyber threats to fintech platforms rise, compliance with these regulations is important to building trust with consumers and avoiding expensive data breaches.

8.3.3 Regulatory Sandboxes and Fintech Innovation

A regulatory sandbox is a controlled environment wherein fintech companies can test their products and services in the presence of regulators but are not bound by the full traditional regulatory requirements. This serves as a sandbox environment to allow innovation by fintech firms while ensuring the risk being posed to consumers and the financial system is not fully exposed. This concept is most beneficial for new market entrants, given that it offers an allowance for experimenting with edge technologies such as blockchain, AI, and digital currencies and is closely monitored by regulators and their guidance.

So far, several countries have created and launched regulatory sandboxes that make fintech innovation more feasible, including in the U.K., Singapore, and Australia. Therefore, it becomes possible for a business to pilot its offer in a few customers with much-reduced compliance requirements than full-scale launches to assure themselves that their product can work without placing the customer at unnecessary risk. Regulatory sandboxes provide an avenue through which the regulators gain a better understanding of these emerging fintech technologies to enable them in designing the future policies and regulations. The role of regulatory sandboxes in promoting innovation as well as a balance between technological advancement and consumer protection will probably rise with further evolution of fintech.

8.4 REGULATORY COMPLIANCE AUTOMATION

Role of Technology in Automating Compliance Tasks

In the financial services and Insurtech industries, it is a day-to-day and complex task for businesses to be up to speed with changing regulations. Because of this, the adoption of technology to automate the compliance process has become imperative for companies. This streamlines the compliance management and reduces manual errors, enhancing efficiency while keeping track of regulatory change, ensuring the organization remains compliant with reporting requirements, and managing risk. For instance, using technology, business organizations can track the status compliance and point out potential problems. As soon as possible, subsequent corrections can be taken into effect without relying upon inherent, paper-based processes, prone to human errors.

Automation technology also encompasses automated data collection and processing used in compliance reporting. It enables companies to embed their regulatory frameworks into the automation systems so that they have compliance with the legal requirements and reporting in a prompt manner, thus avoiding penalties and fines and reputational loss. Moreover, through automation tools, audit trails may be collected to ensure transparency in the compliance process.

8.4.1 Automation Compliance Tools and Platforms

It would become increasingly in-demand compliance automation tools and platforms that simplify business navigation within this increasingly complex regulatory requirements landscape. From monitoring tracking on updates on regulations right to the full automation of some specific KYC, AML, and even a data protection law functionality, these compliance tools attend the needs of compliance with regards to a business's affairs. These reporting, risk assessment, and policy management platforms providing automated solutions for firms with regards to staying compliant as required by regulation can minimize the extent that manual intervention might be needed.

These tools not only provide operational efficiency but also enable companies to track and record compliance activities, promoting both transparency and security in compliance. Most of the platforms are cloud-based, which makes them scalable and flexible. This is of most use to businesses within very fast-changing industries, such as fintech and Insurtech. The advantage also lies in seeing all compliance functions on a single platform and taking all proactive steps to meet all those regulations.

8.4.2 AI/ML for Compliance

AI and ML are increasingly being embedded into compliance automation tools because they enhance the abilities and make compliance processes smarter and more intelligent. For example, AI can quickly determine patterns and predict the type of risk better than anything else. For instance, AI can be applied for suspicious transactions in the services of financial institutions with an aim to flag suspicious fraud in real-time through AML compliance.

Such learning machines further improve compliance as systems continually learn from the new arrival of data and, by doing so, further hone the capabilities of the system to identify new emerging non-compliance patterns. For instance, such technologies might be used for automatically issuing reports that track regulations as they occur in real time and make checks on whether business practices are in compliance with any recent legal mandates. Over time, this will increasingly help in terms of savings in the overall cost incurred for compliance owing to automatic repetition of these tasks; hence, reduced manual overhead.

8.4.3 Benefits and Challenges in Automating Compliance Functions

There are certain benefits while automating these compliance functions. Automation lessens time, effort, and cost that organization needs to absorb to adhere to the legal requirements they are supposed to, in theory. Automation also has the benefit of being not reliant so much on the processes being done manually in terms of avoiding human errors, therefore reporting is also uncomplicated. Additionally, due to not missing recent updates, automation will assure an organization will be always on top of things while, at the same time, useful to ensure proper distribution of resources by concentrating on higher-valued tasks without neglecting its legal compliance.

Even, however, there are disadvantages when automating compliance. One of the concerns is that the technology has to be customized to certain regulatory environments, as various regions have different rules and requirements. Compliance automation tools must be flexible enough to handle jurisdictional differences with consistency and accuracy in the data. Businesses also need to address cybersecurity risks by relying on automated systems that handle sensitive data. The system malfunctions or data breaches could be a direct undermining of the compliance that automation seeks to achieve. These technologies are capital-intensive, and businesses must make sure that the tools adopted are in line with their broad operational goals and regulatory obligations.

Despite these challenges, continued innovation in AI, ML, and cloud-based solutions should keep driving growth and adoption of compliance automation within the spaces of Insurtech and fintech and make it easier for the company to manage its ever more complex regulatory environment more efficiently and securely.

8.5 REGTECH: REGULATORY TECHNOLOGY

What is RegTech and What's its Place in Modern Fintech?

RegTech or, in full words, Regulatory Technology refers to technology for the more effective and less costly automation of processes, which is important to regulatory compliance. Of special relevance to fintech is that the world in financial services is becoming regulated fast and the regulations about their activity are really tricky to interpret. Therefore, there exists very heavy regulation in the financial industry including regulation even at things as basic as customer identification to anti-money laundering; these are high compliance issues for fintech firms. What RegTech does is navigates the companies through the difficulties by using automation, big data analytics, artificial intelligence, and blockchain technology monitoring reports in real time with respect to compliance.

RegTech is an important element in the fintech space because the more complex regulations are, the more important it is. It allows companies to react more quickly to changes in regulatory requirements, reduces risk exposure due to non-compliance, and lowers the costs of operations through the streamlining of human resource-intensive processes. A platform whose capabilities include streamlining its reporting to regulatory authorities and compliance metric tracking as well as audit management, then RegTech is an efficient facilitator of trust in stability in the fintech market for businesses which hold that they should always maintain an upper hand of its legal obligations while still innovative.

8.5.1 Key Components of the RegTech Solutions such as KYC, AML, Fraud Detection

RegTech solutions are a group of several components that are designed to tackle the specific regulatory challenges faced by fintech companies. Among the most common and most important components are:

Know Your Customer (KYC) Know your customer refers to identification of a customer to curtail fraud, money laundering, and financing for terrorism. RegTech solutions automate the KYC process using AI and machine learning to verify documents, conduct background checks, and track the behaviour of customers. Not only does it speed up the onboarding process for new customers but also it is compliant with AML.

Anti-Money Laundering: AML is a compliance requirement of any financial institution. RegTech solutions allow fintech firms to track transactions for suspicious activities, analyze patterns, and raise red flags for money laundering operations. The automated AML systems are using big data analytics and AI for continuous real-time monitoring of transactions, high-risk client identification, and alerting of suspicious behaviour.

Fraud Detection: The systems for RegTech also play an important role in fraud prevention, where these systems analyze transactional data for signs of fraudulent activities. These solutions apply the use of machine learning algorithms to identify atypical spending behaviour or unauthorized access in an account, and sometimes these can trigger alerts that may require further investigation. These platforms by applying predictive analytics and AI ensure that fraud happens even before it happens to avoid loss of finance. They thus increase customer safety.

Some of these modules have often been included in a seamless system to make financial institutions comply with standards while ensuring a high degree of efficiency and reduced human error.

8.5.2 Cases of Successful Implementation of RegTech

Many fintech companies and financial institutions have successfully implemented RegTech solutions to improve compliance processes. For example, the company TransferWise changed its name to Wise, and applied tools of RegTech to the process of KYC and AML. By means of such automated customer verification systems as real-time transaction monitoring, Wise complies with the international regulations, reduces the time and resources wasted on the checks.

Another successful case is Revolut, which is developing a digital banking platform using RegTech to catch frauds and remain in AML compliance. The company has, therefore integrated AI-based solutions into the platform in analysing real-time transaction data in order to detect suspicious patterns and lessen the financial risks of associated crimes. Thus, through this implementation, Revolut was able to provide safe services for customers all around the globe.

Lemonade, an insurer digitally, has applied RegTech for KYC and fraud detection. With AI-driven identity-checking systems and fraud-detection algorithms, it has streamlined the onboarding process and reduced frauds while making insurance more accessible and affordable for customers.

Such case studies are demonstrations of how RegTech can help the fintech firms in the fulfilment of regulatory requirements besides increasing operational efficiency, decreasing costs, and gaining customers' trust.

8.5.3 Future Trends in RegTech and Its Impact on the Fintech Landscape

Emerging trends appear to promise a good future for RegTech and possibly shape its role in the fintech landscape. Rapidly emerging is the advent of artificial intelligence and machine learning in RegTech services. Such technologies are seen to propel more powerful, sophisticated predictive analytics, the real-time detection of risks, and automation of the process of compliance. Thus, as AI and ML algorithms keep improving, RegTech will become more aggressive in identifying and mitigating compliance risks long before they themselves become issues.

Another trend is the use of blockchain technology for compliance purposes. The immutable ledger system in blockchain can be used for secure and transparent tracking of transactions, audit trails, and KYC processes. This will ensure that financial transactions have more integrity and the risk of fraud or manipulation will be much lower, especially in the payments, lending, and insurance sectors.

Increased regulatory requirements and complexity in regulations are going to require the increased demand for the automation of regulatory reporting. RegTech platforms will be offering automatic reporting solutions in the times to come and make compliance easier for financial institutions under various regional and jurisdictional regulatory requirements.

The emergence of collaborative RegTech ecosystems can be expected to transform access to compliance solutions by the fintech companies. They are expected to bring more strategic partnerships between startups and traditional financial institutions with technologies that combine to create customised integrated, scalable, and business-specific or geographic market-specific compliance solutions.

As these trends evolve, RegTech will be critical in allowing fintech companies to scale, innovate, and operate in an environment of high regulation. Its impact will cut across the entire fintech landscape and improve not only compliance but also operational efficiency, security, and customer experience.

8.6 AUTOMATION IN RISK MANAGEMENT

Role of Automation in Risk Assessment and Mitigation

Modern risk management is based on automation in respect of process streamlining, increased accuracy and efficiency. Traditional risk assessment is time-consuming and error-prone because of the dependency of manual data gathering, analysis, and decision-making. In this regard, automation has significantly improved the ability of financial institutions and insurers to evaluate risk much better as it sustains on sophisticated algorithms, artificial intelligence, and machine learning for quick and accurate analysis of mammoth data. With the availability of automated systems, the use of credit scores, financial health, market conditions, and behavioural patterns could thus be assessed to provide an all-inclusive, up-to-date risk profile.

It allows a business the opportunity to look at areas where risks could develop before they do so and, therefore, implement mitigating steps. A few of these risks involve marking high-risk customers, monitoring odd transactions, and also foretelling changes in markets. The speed that comes from automating the risk assessment process has, in return, insured that the decisions are done based on data rather than personal bias and increases consistency in risk management practices.

8.6.1 Automated Risk Monitoring Tools

This will enable constant assessment and monitoring of risks through various business functions. The tools, based on AI and machine learning algorithms, analyze the real-time data streams coming from different sources, including financial markets, transaction histories, or customer behaviour patterns, in order to identify emerging risks or vulnerabilities. The automation of risk monitoring allows organizations to respond more quickly and effectively to threats, thereby decreasing the time it takes to detect and address potential problems.

For example, automated tools can allow banks to monitor market and liquidity risks in real-time; the same tool will help insurers monitor the claims frequency and severity so the actual underwriting problems are identifiable. Such systems will connect data from external sources like economic indicators or updates about regulations to illustrate an entirely comprehensive risk exposure view. Risk monitoring in real-time enables a company to take corrective actions faster, which can save enormous resources and prevent damage to their reputation or bottom line.

8.6.2 Real-Time Reporting and Automated Alerts for Regulatory Breaches

Real-time reporting and automated alerts are the key to compliance and avoiding regulatory violations. It is, therefore, imperative for financial services as well as insurance companies to keep abreast of changes in compliance requirements since regulations change constantly and active regulators keep updating them. Thanks to automation, the firms continuously monitor their business and keep producing real-time reports concerning key risk indicators like capital adequacy or any transaction irregularities ascertaining that the standards are met to the letter but this doesn't happen under human watchful eyes.

Automated alert systems alert managers and compliance officers the moment particular thresholds are breached, say a sudden spiking in transactions, shift in market conditions, or failure to comply with certain regulations. This enables organizations to take corrective measures promptly, reducing the likelihood of non-compliance fines and reputational damage. For instance, an investment company could be alerted when its customer's transactions are running above what is usual such that they can then review the possible frauds; it will therefore need such a process to be automated so that firms can stay better within limits and thus minimize their level of risk to regulation.

8.6.3 Use of integrated automated risk management systems with fintech

For further simplification of the processes of risk identification, risk assessment, and mitigation, automated risk management systems are connected to fintech platforms. Automation in the risk management process is advantageous in the operation of highly dynamic environments in which most fintech platforms operate. In general, fintech platforms can employ a number of automated risk management tools: fraud detection algorithms, credit scoring models, predictive analytics, and so forth. The integration will allow fintech companies to analyze risk in real-time, change strategies based on an ever-changing market and user behaviour and requirements of regulatory systems.

For example, an automated lending digital platform can use its systems to assess the creditworthiness of any loan applicant using social media activity or mobile phone usage as alternative data, while constantly monitoring the loan portfolio for early signs of default. On one side, blockchain-based platforms empower the real-time tracking as well as validation of transaction and curb frauds, even mistakes in the overall business process. With Fintech and automation altogether, businesses help improve its procedures regarding the management of risks and cut down operation expenses besides being able to deliver maximum security with greater front-end performance towards customers. This synergy between fintech and automated risk management truly represents a great industry revolution in that firms can no only identify and mitigate more precisely, but also fully smooth out operations.

8.7 IMPACT OF AUTOMATION ON COMPLIANCE AND GOVERNANCE

How Automation Enhances Compliance and Governance Work

Automation is revolutionizing work in compliance and governance in industries like insurance, finance, and health care-complex and always evolving laws. This is the gateway through which such organizations achieve routine compliance activities in a manner that their reporting for data, risk assessment, and audit trails will be to the required set of regulations. Through automation, some tools are in place with the capability of tracking or monitoring real-time compliance and alerting the organizations regarding certain violations or issues before them becoming costly mistakes. Automated systems can even integrate with regulatory databases where policies and procedures are made to always be current with the latest legal or industry standards, thereby sharply reducing the risk of becoming non-compliant.

For example, automation enables the firms to better serve regulatory bodies with easy collection and reportage of data such that their data protection rules such as GDPR is adhered well. Also, it brings to its attention instances when policy or claims may have fallen short of complying within the required needs such that corrective measures are put forward in time. This would mean organizations could observe to be compliant while governance frames are clear, effective and efficient.

8.7.1 Reduce Human Error and Bias Through Automation

Human error and bias are the persistent challenges to regulatory compliance and governance. Errors of data entry, misinterpretation of rules, and inconsistency in decisions can be prevented through automation. All such issues can be done away with when most of the human elements in routine work are taken out, thus having an accurate and consistent outcome. Automated systems observe strict guidelines and rules, which means carrying out compliance activities to the letter and as required by regulatory requirements without deviation.

Automation also minimizes decision-making bias. The consideration of risk, reports, or opinions may contain a few subjective biases that exist in any traditional system which are imparted by the compliance officer or auditor. However, automation makes choices based on data-driven rules that culminate in equitable and non-biased results. This can go a long way in businesses such as insurance underwriting or financial auditing where absolute objectivity in decision making is quite crucial in regard to compliance with regulatory law and moral governance.

8.7.2 Cost Savings and Efficiency Improvements

The greatest potential benefit of automation in compliance and governance is cost savings and efficiency improvements. Compliance work consumes such time and resources in manual data entry, auditing, and reporting. There would be less demand for considerable human labour; this is why compliance teams may be focused on more critical work, such as strategic decision-making or managing risks. With the automated routine processes, businesses function more effectively and save what would otherwise be channelled into other business-related activities or invested in innovations.

In fact, automation prevents the expensive fines and penalties as a result of non-compliance. It ensures regulatory requirements are met; the process is done consistently and in real-time, by which way it avoids potential errors or omissions because of which non-compliance usually results. In the long run, it would save money for an organization because this approach avoids pricey legal problems and reputational damage.

8.7.3 The Balance between Automation and Human Oversight

Many are the benefits of automation, and at the same time it is of high importance; therefore, balance between automation and oversight of human beings to respect regulatory compliance. Automation deals with repetitive and rule-based tasks efficiently. Decision-making and judgment calls accompanied by exceptions require human oversight. For instance, automation might be able to process huge amounts of data to declare the presence of patterns or signal potential compliance issues but would leave the interpretation of nuances and strategic decisions and those situations that fall outside standard protocols to a compliance officer. Furthermore, dynamic environments in regulations necessitate human oversight to ensure that changes in laws, policies, or business operations are integrated into automated systems. Therefore, in terms of effective governance, one has to balance automated procedures with the human element-a role that the latter is likely to play in important oversight to ensure compliance or issues that cannot be altogether solved by automation. Hence, the marriage of high-efficiency automation with sound judgment and expertise from oversight is likely to make firms achieve a strong and highly resilient compliance framework.

8.8 CHALLENGES AND RISKS IN REGULATORY COMPLIANCE AUTOMATION

Legal and Ethical Challenges in Automating Compliance Functions

There are a few legal and ethical challenges companies face when they increasingly use automation to make regulatory compliance easier. Among these compliance functions automated are the algorithms and the AI systems that interpret and execute the regulatory rules. Sometimes, however, such systems will miss the subtlety of legal requirements. That will mean making the systems to automate and then understand the regulations to their proper level of meaning and apply them uniformly to any business operation. A single problem in the compliance automation system could then result in an event like failure in classifying a transaction or possibly missing a new regulation resulting in legal consequences, though very costly to include a possible fine or reputational damage.

There are some ethical issues with accountability and fair treatment in automating compliance functions. For instance, automated systems may unwittingly perpetuate bias where such systems depend on historical data that would have been influenced by prevailing prejudices. There is a risk of businesses becoming too reliant onautomation, which may lead them to overlook human judgment and consequently miss potential legal or ethical issues that a human expert might have caught. This needs to be balanced between the risks of automation and the use of human judgment.

8.8.1 Adapting automation with changing laws and regulatory uncertainty

The most significant problem of handling automation of regulatory compliance relates to uncertainty and constant evolution in the regulations. Rules and the regulatory framework evolve constantly and are usually responses to changes in technology, industry practices, or newly emerging risks. For instance, with cryptocurrency or AI-driven services emerging in financial industries, there is always something new that regulators need to adapt and introduce new requirements for compliance.

These constant changes can be quite tough to deal with for automated compliance systems. Companies must continually update their algorithms and procedures to be in compliance with new legislation, which can be an operational burden and costly. There is also diversity in the regulatory environment within jurisdictions, and this only adds another layer of complication to the global companies' need to adapt automation tools to meet the various requirements of the locality. One of the issues the business will have to face as long as it depends on automation for compliance is keeping track of regulatory changes, given that the pace at which they change differs from region to region.

8.8.2 Data Privacy Concerns and Security Risks Management

Data privacy and security happen to be at the centre of most regulatory compliance frameworks. The EU has the General Data Protection Regulation (GDPR), and California enacted the California Consumer Privacy Act (CCPA). The company's risk being highly exposed to data privacy issues while handling sensitive data, which is increasingly being automated in financial, healthcare, and other regulated industries. The automated compliance systems rely on large datasets, which include personally identifiable information (PII), customer records, and other sensitive data. Failure to secure such data properly, either through weak encryption or poor access controls or vulnerabilities within the automation software, means that huge breaches in terms of data and even law suits can be the resulting outcome.

In addition, when compliance processes are automated sometimes, a hazy situation arises in which people become confused and ask questions regarding who should get hold of sensitive data after things get haywire. This gives firms an assurance that the implementation of the automation systems, where it is robustly secured with encryption technologies, such sensitive data anonymized, and controlled access, may ensure a curb on malicious practices. Audits and vulnerability testing can help in safety risks in keeping and compliance to ever-changing data protection legislations.

8.8.3 Transparency and accountability in the automated compliance systems

There exists transparency and accountability in employing the automated compliance systems. One of the dangers of automation is the opaqueness of making decisions, especially complex AI-driven systems. This tends to leave behind traces as to how decisions were made and which part of the system was responsible for the mistake. Such non-transparency leads to a lack of accountability because firms are not sure who is actually responsible - the developers, the algorithms, or perhaps the inputs of data.

Transparency in compliance systems must, therefore become a major priority for such businesses in order to avoid such risks. This would, among other things ensure that all system activity leaves a clean audit trail, so that whatever decision the automated system makes will leave space for documenting it, and mechanisms are put in place to provide for human intervention and oversight when automated process are at their most prevalent. If the decisions made by algorithms in designing the automated systems can be understood and traced, then transparency issues are mitigated and accountability takes on more force.

8.9 FUTURE OF REGULATORY COMPLIANCE AND AUTOMATION IN FINTECH

Emerging Technologies, Specifically AI and Blockchain, on Compliance Frameworks

The future of the fintech sector will see compliance frameworks change significantly due to evolving technologies including AI and blockchain. With the ability of AI to have machine learning and predictive analytics capabilities, fintech companies can enhance their compliance processes by automating tasks such as fraud detection, risk assessment, and transaction monitoring. AI-driven tools can process vast amounts of transaction data in real time and look for patterns that may signal suspicious behaviour, keeping the company ahead of the curve in terms of compliance requirements. It is possible for AI to ensure fintech firms are always compliant with evolving regulatory requirements through the automatic adjustment of policies and procedures as per regulatory changes. Blockchain can revolutionize compliance by providing a transparent, immutable ledger for financial transactions. With its decentralized nature, blockchain presents the possibility of building a secure, verifiable record-keeping that it will make it much easier to track and audit the activity of financial compliance under regulatory requirements. This will significantly reduce complexity in audits and reporting to the regulatory agency since all transactions could be recorded on a tamper-proof system. Blockchain can also make processes of Know Your Customer and Anti-Money Laundering much more efficient and safer, while allowing easier cross-platform identity verification in compliance with privacy laws.

8.9.1 Role of Automation in a Much More Decentralized Financial System

As the financial ecosystem goes increasingly decentralized, automation would take more prominent roles over regulatory compliance. In DeFi, by which smart contracts and blockchain help offer financial services and exclude middlemen, this tends to accelerate transactions with improved efficiency. However, the same raises oversight issues in that no central authority may enforce such compliance.

To do this, automation within DeFi can enforce regulatory requirements programmatically, directly in the smart contracts themselves. For example, automated compliance protocols may guarantee that relevant transactions will meet compliance with specific regulations such as KYC and AML without a human. This way, smart contracts are able to execute automatic checks on the compliance so that regulatory requirements can be followed in an uninterrupted and timely manner over time. In this way, automation makes efficiency possible but ensures that compliance continually occurs in a decentralized regime, thus doing away with the threats of violating regulatory requirements.

8.9.2 Future Regulatory Environment in Fintech

The regulation environment of the future may be integrated, adaptive and global. In the not-so-distant future, when fintech continues to blossom and evolve into more multifaceted technologies, new approaches in regulatory policies may be implemented in a collaborative and amenable style. Regulations will change with new business models in blockchain, DeFi, and AI-driven financial services. Governments and regulatory bodies should keep abreast of the speed at which technology changes and provide frameworks that could adapt in real-time, without hindering innovation.

We could also see increased attention towards global regulatory harmonization since most fintech companies are working across borders. With the increasing efforts of firms to scale across geographies and with the rising complexity of multiple legal systems, pressure for homogenous regulations would rise. In addition, there would be an increased trend of “regulatory sandboxes” — environments where fintech firms can test innovative products under relaxed regulatory scrutiny, with the intention of refining regulations for broader application. Lastly, regulators will likely concentrate on consumer protection, ensuring that new technologies do not bring unknown risks or abuse.

8.9.3 Collaboration between Fintech Companies, Regulators, and Technology Providers

As fintech continues to evolve, collaboration between fintech companies, regulators, and technology providers will be quite important in creating a sustainable regulatory ecosystem. Fintech companies will increasingly work with regulators to ensure that products and services are in compliance with relevant legislation while maintaining innovation. This means, while technology vendors are concentrated on specific areas such as AI, blockchain, and cloud computing, there would also be a lot for technology vendors to play the key role and they should try creating tools that assist the fintech firms with their undertakings, which simultaneously keeps up requirements for regulation.

This might be achieved through better co-operation in building solutions toward compliance or collaboration toward standards by the industry with regards to the new technologies. The regulators can enter partnerships with fintech firms to be made aware of the new emerging technologies and risks that they pose. For instance, through such partnerships, fintech firms can educate regulators about how AI algorithms make decisions on lending and insurance issues, while the latter provide feedback to them regarding areas of knowledge gaps in their regulatory systems. That would keep the fintech business innovative and responsible since, through the regulation of both the consumer and the money markets, its framework stands by the well-being of everyone involved.

www.ingramcontent.com/pod-product-compliance
Lightning Source LLC
LaVergne TN
LVHW070936160826
845679LV00021B/1813

9798897449170